D0065229

RKO CLASSIC SCREENPLAYS

(Wagonmaster)

Directed by: John Ford
Screenplay by: Frank Nugent
and
Patrick Ford

An Andrew Velez Book

FREDERICK UNGAR PUBLISHING CO.
New York

Published by arrangement with RKO General, Inc.

PUBLISHER'S NOTE:
This is the complete final screenplay for the RKO film.
The movie as released may differ from the screenplay
in some respects.

Printed in Great Britain
by Biddles of Guildford

ISBN 0-8044-6166-X

INTRODUCTION

Andrew Sinclair

Wagonmaster is John Ford's tribute to the Mormon pioneers. Made for his own production company Argosy in 1949, it showed his belief in old American values. Ford had become attached to the Mormons when they were serving as his cavalry in *She Wore a Yellow Ribbon*. He admired the way they would rise at six o'clock in the morning and work hard until sundown. It was their religion and their pride. So he wanted to make a film which explained how such people came to be. He found a true story about their coming to the West.

Shot without stars and without fanfare, *Wagonmaster* was Ford's response to a world of increasing complexity and a tribute to the abiding values of courage and endurance, loyalty, and faith in troubled times. The plot resembles *Stagecoach,* with a group of people traveling toward a promised land through a series of dangers. In both films there is a whore with a heart of gold named after a Western city—Denver takes over from Dallas—and a tough-gentle guardian, with Ben Johnson as Travis Blue playing John Wayne's old character of the Ringo Kid. But *Wagonmaster* is more episodic and relaxed, its unity the moving picture of the wagons rolling or straining across the continent in sequences of continuous effort, not the mere device of a single Concord coach pulling the protagonists from conflict to climax to conclusion.

The wagons are, indeed, the film; their master is John Ford. For once his images approach those of his only rival, Eisenstein. The screen is filled with moving lines that climb it or slash it, curve away or strain down it, change direction or criss-cross over it. The dialectic of movement that was the invention of the early Russian cinema appears in *Wagonmaster*. Ford is at the reins and in the cutting room, working with his daughter and Jack Murray to show in edited pictures the long traverse to the pioneer dream.

Wagonmaster is also a return to the simpler world of Ford's early Westerns, not to the religious symbolism of *Three Godfathers,* but to the sweat and hardship, detail, and dirt of the lives of the settlers and outlaws. When the Navajos appear, they are the rightful guardians of the land, friendly to the Mormons because they seem only petty thieves. But when the bandit Cleggs appear, they are as villainous as Lucifer himself, old Uncle

Shiloh with his appalling nephews as irredeemable as any black-masked desperado from a melodrama.

If there is a human hero in the film it is Ward Bond, playing the Mormon leader, Elder Wiggs, a man of surpassing faith in God and in himself. He likes to interpret what he thinks the wagon train should do as the will of the Lord. When Travers points out to him that he and the Lord seem to think alike, he replies, "Not always, son—sometimes He takes a little persuadin'." He is Ford's essential hero, enduring and tricky, religious and wry, who takes to violence only as the last resort.

Oddly enough, Elder Wiggs is also an outcast, along with his people. They have been outlawed from American society because of plural marriage, as well as other imagined sins. The irony of *Wagonmaster* is that the Mormons, themselves the victims of prejudice, are prejudiced in their turn. They fear Travis and his friend as Gentiles, and they despise Denver and her traveling stage companions as sinners. Like *Stagecoach,* the film is also a comedy of social prejudice as well as a hymn of praise for community in adversity, bound together by folksongs that seem to flow as easily as the sequences and the wagon wheels rolling across the waste.

When the Mormon caravan finally reaches the last stretch of water before the promised land and the music swells in triumph to the tune of "Shall We Gather at the River?" the confusion of the actions of men and the hope of God are perfect, and the earthly way seems to become the heavenly purpose. As Ward Bond has already said in Elder Wiggs's crafty words, "The way I see it, the Lord went to an awful lot of trouble to put these people in our way . . . and if I was *Him*, I wouldn't want anybody messin' up *my* plans."

Wagonmaster is a triumph of Ford's planning: direct, simple, clear, necessary. It ranks with *Stagecoach* and *The Man Who Shot Liberty Valence* in its admirable crafting and spare evocation of the spirit of the American West.

CAST:

Travis	Ben Johnson
Denver	Joanne Dru
Sandy	Harry Carey, Jr.
Wiggs	Ward Bond

with:

Charles Kemper	Alan Mowbray
Jane Darwell	Ruth Clifford
Russell Simpson	Kathleen O'Malley
James Arness	Fred Libby
Mickey Simpson	Hank Worden
Motiva Castaneda	Francis Ford
Jim Thorpe	Cliff Lyons

Don Summers

CREDITS:

Written by	Frank Nugent
	Patrick Ford
Directed by	John Ford
Produced by	Argosy Pictures Corporation
Musical Score by	Richard Hageman

Songs:

    "Shadows in the Dust"
    "Song of the Wagonmaster"
    "Wagons West"
    "Chuckawalla Swing"

Words and Music by	Stan Jones
Recorded by	The Sons Of The Pioneers
Director of Photography	Bert Glennon, A.S.C.
Art Director	James Basevi
Associate Producer	Lowell Farrell
Film Editor	Jack Murray
Second Unit Photography	Archie Stout, A.S.C
Sound	Frank Webster
	Clem Portman
Assistant Director	Wingate Smith
Costume Research	D. R. O. Hatswell
Men's Wardrobe	Wes Jeffries
Women's Wardrobe	Adele Parmenter
Make-up	Don Cash
Hair Dresser	Anna Malin
Special Effects	Jack Caffee
Properties	Jack Golconda
Set Decorator	Joe Kish
Distributed by	RKO Radio Pictures, Inc.

WAGONMASTER

FADE IN

FULL SHOT—CRYSTAL CITY—DAY

Four riders come at an easy lope along the trail at the outskirts of Crystal City, Utah. They are the Cleggs—Uncle Shiloh and his nephews, Jesse, Reese, and Floyd. As they approach the camera we see them for what they are—Arkansas white trash, inbred, amoral, animal in their cunning and their cruelty.

Uncle Shiloh is the head of the clan, a man about 55, with a stubble of grey whisker and a drying trickle of tobacco juice down the corner of his mouth. Shiloh is a slippery-tongued, thoroughly evil old man with a strong clan feeling.

Floyd, oldest of the boys, is the two-gunman, the pistol fighter—a lean panther of a man with a panther's taste for blood and its unconscious grace in his every movement. His eyes are watchful.

Jesse is the butcher—a fighter whose weapon is the double-barreled shotgun. Unlike Floyd, Jesse doesn't believe in challenge or any of the refinements of the frontier's code duello: he kills from cover or from behind.

Reese is the muscle man, the gouger and the kicker. He has two weaknesses: one is woman, the other his mind.

1

*As the horsemen pass the camera it pans slightly to pick up a sign on
the outskirts of town. It hangs tipsily by one broken link and the
lettering is already faded and weathered. It reads:*

Watch

CRYSTAL CITY

Grow

REVERSE ANGLE—MAIN STREET, CRYSTAL CITY

*The four horsemen slow their pace slightly as they proceed down
the broad, dusty main street of the town. It is the typical 1880 ghost
town in the making—with mongrel dogs drowsing or scratching
fleas in the street, a few horses hitched to the rails outside the saloon
and the frame Crystal City Hotel. The Cleggs rein in before the
wooden steps and sidewalk of the Wells-Fargo Office.*

EXTERIOR WELLS-FARGO OFFICE

*The Cleggs dismount and, leaving Reese with the horses, Shiloh
and Jesse take rifle and shotgun respectively from their saddle
holsters and follow Floyd up the steps and into the Wells-Fargo
office.*

INTERIOR WELLS-FARGO OFFICE

*Shooting over the heads of the Cleggs as they enter the office. Two
clerks are behind the counter, two or three other men in front of it.
An open express box is being filled with packets of greenbacks.
Suddenly one of the clerks looks up to see the newcomers. His eyes
widen and his hands start reaching. The other men—stage drivers,
etc.—turn and then they, too, reach. The Cleggs advance and Uncle
Shiloh starts scooping the money packets into a cloth bag. Not a
word has been said. The Cleggs start backing out.*
*Just as they reach the door, one of the clerks whips up a gun and
snaps a shot, which hits Uncle Shiloh in the left shoulder.*
*As Shiloh staggers, Floyd—who has not drawn his guns—makes a
lightning-like draw and fires.*
*The gun drops from the clerk's shattered arm and he stands
helpless... his eyes widening with terror.*

2

MEDIUM CLOSE ON SHILOH AND JESSE

SHILOH: *(in tones of gentle reproach)* Wish you hadn't done that, son.
He extends his right hand toward Jesse.
SHILOH: Gimme the shotgun, Jesse.

MEDIUM CLOSE—THE CLERK
As the other men draw away from him, accentuating his loneliness.
The clerk takes a hopeless backward step toward the wall—and
then the shotgun blasts. Both barrels!

EXTERIOR WELLS-FARGO OFFICE AND MAIN STREET
Shiloh, Jesse, and Floyd back out of the Wells-Fargo office, joining
Reese. They mount and spur their horses out of town by the same
road they had come in. They fling a few random shots behind them
as men start running out of buildings onto the street.

CUT TO:

EXTERIOR—OPEN COUNTRY—DAY
A mile or so outside Crystal City, two young horse-traders are
driving their remuda of horses toward the town. They are Travis
Houston Blue of Texas and Sandy Owens of Abilene, Kansas.
Travis is a calm-eyed, easy-going, competent young wrangler
whose philosophy may be summed up in one line: "I mind my own
business and keep a sharp eye out for snakes." He is clearly senior
partner of the firm.
Sandy is carrot-topped, good-natured yet hot-tempered. His
clothing—although as dusty and travel-stained as Travis's—is a bit
more dashing and colorful. Sandy is an innocent constantly trying
to be mistaken for a gay caballero.
Sandy is driving a horse-trader's cart—a stout buckboard with an
improvised cover of tattered canvas, with pots and pans hanging
over the side, a water keg lashed to the tail—in effect a small-scale
chuckwagon.
Travis ranges alongside, handling his mount with the effortless
grace of the born horseman, and keeping his eye on a well-bunched
string of Navajo ponies.

3

Sandy is singing some cowboy ballad, but he breaks off in the middle of a bar as Travis rides in close.

MOVING ON TRAVIS AND SANDY

SANDY: *(optimistic mood)* Way I figger, Travis . . . these ponies ought to bring thirty dollars a head.

Travis merely gives him an amused glance, but says nothing.

SANDY: An' twelve head at thirty dollars comes to three hundred and twenty!

TRAVIS: Three sixty!

SANDY: *(pleased surprise)* It does! . . . Better yet . . . And divided by two, why, that makes . . .

He bogs down.

SANDY: Um . . . why, that makes a tidy sum!

TRAVIS: And now if you'll subtract the twenty you owe me from that tidy sum, you'll have a hundred and sixty left . . .

SANDY: *(happily)* I will? . . . Why, that's not bad for four months' work . . . not bad at all . . .

He resumes his singing with new enthusiasm, but breaks off at the sound of distant shots, at the approaching drum of hooves.
The horses in the remuda begin acting up and Travis has his hands full controlling them.

LONG SHOT—OPEN COUNTRY—DAY

With Travis and Sandy in foreground, the Cleggs appear in the distance riding at a gallop and firing at an unseen posse. The Cleggs' course is toward the horse-traders' wagon, but when they see it they veer slightly. The posse comes into view behind them—clearly outdistanced and obviously in a vain pursuit.

ANGLE ON HORSE-CART

Sandy reaches back into the wagon and half pulls out a rifle. Travis spurs his horse between Sandy and the Cleggs.

TRAVIS: *(urgently)* Never mind that!

And he swings his horse away and back toward the plunging animals in the remuda, forcing them back into their former compact bunch. Once again Travis's splendid horsemanship is featured.

4

LONG SHOT
The Cleggs vanish over a dip in the hills.

ANOTHER ANGLE
On the posse as it reins in at an arm signal from the marshal, clearly abandoning the pursuit. Then at a lope, the posse approaches the horse-traders. The marshal is an angry man and only waits until he is within hailing distance to let the boys know it.

MARSHAL: What's the matter with you fellas?

FULL SHOT AT WAGON
As the marshal and one or two posse members ride close. Travis dismounts.

MARSHAL: *(fuming)* Chase 'em right into your laps 'n you set here 'n let 'em go!... Coulda taken a shot at 'em anyways!... Them was the Cleggs!

Travis seems not to have heard the marshal's tirade, but has been standing studying the marshal's horse with a shrewd trader's eye. Now he comes closer to the animal, feeling of its haunches, checking hocks and withers, perhaps "grunting" it. The marshal doesn't submit patiently to this scrutiny, but reins his horse from side to side.

TRAVIS: *(as he starts this—in a very casual tone)* Wasn't our fight, Marshal...

MARSHAL: *(angrily)* Yeah? Well, maybe you don't know I got a right to arrest you for aidin' 'n abettin'!... Law says it's the duty of every... GIT AWAY FROM MY HORSE!... duty of every male citizen to... to...

He breaks off peering, interested in spite of himself, as Travis goes to his horse's head and opens its mouth to study its teeth.

TRAVIS: *(reflectively)* Pretty fair... Tell you what, Marshal... I'll trade you that bay gelding and five dollars for your horse.

MARSHAL: *(testily)* Didn't come out here to swap horses!

The marshal starts to ride off, moving past Sandy.

SANDY: I thought the Cleggs were operatin' back in Kansas.

MARSHAL: *(sulkily)* Well, they're operatin' in Utah territory now!... But they won't be for long!

The marshal continues away, but Travis calls after him.

5

TRAVIS: I'll make that ten dollars—cash!

The marshal is tempted. He pulls to a stop, hesitates—then his sense of outrage returns.

MARSHALL: Ten, eh?... Well, that's a... *(then angrily)* NO!... Come on, boys.

He and the posse start away.

TRAVIS: *(calling)* See you again, Marshall...

MARSHAL: *(sourly)* Not likely!

As the posse spurs off, Travis stands looking after it with a faint grin.

DISSOLVE

EXTERIOR—MAIN STREET CRYSTAL CITY—DAY

It is a day or two later. Down the street come two men, Jonathan Wiggs and Adam Perkins, followed at a respectful distance by Perkins's pretty daughter, Prudence.

Elder Wiggs is a wiry, grizzled, Mormon man of God, with twinkling eyes, a dry sense of humor and a lamentable habit of semi-profanity which he repents a dozen times a day. God and Jonathan know each other mighty well. Jonathan has given God more hearty laughs than any Saint (Latter Day or otherwise) in the register: we can be sure He has a very special halo reserved for Elder Wiggs—one that will be worn at a slight tilt over one eye.

Brother Perkins is a good man but dull. It is no secret that he is bucking for Bishop.

Prudence is a lissome, bright-eyed, spirited girl, with a mind of her own—qualities obviously inherited from her late mother.

The little party proceeds down the dusty street at a good pace, purposeful and preoccupied and apparently oblivious of the small covey of children following them at a cautious distance with wide eyes and a fearful—but wholly fascinated—curiosity. For these people are Mormons of whom they have heard some awesome things.

Wiggs and Perkins stop and turn off at the place where the horse-traders have made their camp. It is either a corral or an improvised enclosure of rope and stakes (depending on availability) where Sandy and Travis are offering their remuda for sale.

6

EXTERIOR—CORRAL—DAY
As the Mormons approach in the background, Travis is closing a horse trade with the marshal, who is already mounted on the bay gelding he has just acquired. A small knot of townsmen is standing around watching the transaction. Travis counts silver dollars into the marshal's palm.

TRAVIS: . . . ten, eleven, twelve . . . Got yourself a good horse, Marshal. 'Course, he has his own little peculiarities. His own little failin's. Ain't he, Sandy?

Travis winks at Sandy, who cracks his quirt sharply against his boot. The whip-shy bay gelding breaks into a series of back-breaking bucks. The marshal is forced to grab leather as the onlookers guffaw at his discomfiture.

ANOTHER ANGLE
Favoring the onlookers as Wiggs and Perkins push through the group to approach Travis and Sandy. The hearty laughter of the onlookers dwindles and dies at the sight of the Mormons. The men move aside, grudgingly making room for them. Travis and Sandy cannot help but be conscious of the slight chill in the atmosphere. Prudence stays with the Mormons, but somewhat behind them— not intruding on men's affairs. Wiggs turns to Travis as the top man of the partnership.

WIGGS: What are you asking for your horses, mister?

TRAVIS: All of 'em?

WIGGS: Yup.

TRAVIS: *(kiting his price)* Fifty a head.

WIGGS: *(outraged)* FIFTY?! . . . Why, I be go to . . . !

Perkins winces and plucks the elder's coatsleeve.

PERKINS: *(shocked)* Elder Wiggs!

Wiggs turns on him sourly.

WIGGS: But bear's paws, Adam! . . . Fifty dollars! The Lord Hisself'd be apt to say I be go to . . .

Again the threatened profanity shocks Perkins.

PERKINS: *(cautioning finger upraised)* Elder!

WIGGS: *(grudgingly)* All right. I repent my words of wrath . . . *(with renewed anger as he turns back to Travis)* BUT I BE GOSH-DANGED

7

IF I PAY ANY FIFTY! *(more quietly)* Where'd you get your horses, mister?

SANDY: *(truculently)* Meanin' exactly what?

WIGGS: Now keep your shirt on, son. Your face may be homely, but it's honest.

TRAVIS: Caught some ... traded for some ... Navajo country mostly ... southwest of here.

> *Wiggs looks at him with sudden new interest.*

WIGGS: Happen you know the San Juan River country?

SANDY: *(still a little mad)* Yeah, we know it! What about it, Grampaw?

WIGGS: *(flaring)* Don't you grampaw me, you whippersnapper, or I'll fan your britches!

PERKINS: Now, Elder ...

WIGGS: *(regaining control with an effort)* Folks around here say there's no trail through to the San Juan.

TRAVIS: Folks is right.

SANDY: But we been there!

WIGGS: With your *wagon?*

TRAVIS: *(grinning)* That little ole cart's part burro ... it just goes anywhere!

> *Wiggs and Perkins exchange glances, Perkins seeming doubtful, but Wiggs hot on the scent.*

WIGGS: Mind tellin' me if you're drinkin' men?

> *The boys shake their heads.*

SANDY: *(proudly)* Got a brother's a drunkard, though.

WIGGS: Do ya chaw?

> *Again the headshake.*

TRAVIS: Tried it once ...

PERKINS: *(like a D.A.)* Use the words of wrath?

> *Boys look vague, so Wiggs translates.*

WIGGS: He means—do you cuss?

TRAVIS: Only tol'able well ...

WIGGS: Um—we'll let that pass ... You family men?

BOYS: *(in unison)* No, sir ...

> *Wiggs looks at Perkins, who now seems satisfied—although not completely.*

WIGGS: *(coming to point)* How'd you like to sell your horses for fifty a

head—an' mebbe pick up an extra hundred?

TRAVIS: Doin' what?

WIGGS: Wagonmaster, that's what!... Leading our wagons to the San Juan... to a valley the Lord's been reservin' for His people... so we can plough it an' seed it an' make it fruitful in His sight!

Sandy and Travis look at the Mormons with sudden comprehension.

SANDY: You people Mormons?

WIGGS: That's right... That's why I keep my hat on—so my horns don't show! And I got more wives than Solomon himself... least that's what folks say around here... And if they don't say it, they think it...

FIRST MAN: If you don't like it around here...

SECOND MAN: No one's askin' you to stay, mister...

WIGGS: *(earnestly)* We ain't a big party, son... just a handful sent out to mark the trail an' prepare the ground for the ones comin' after... Next summer there's goin' to be a hundred families on the move... and they're countin' on us to have a crop ready for 'em... If we don't they'll starve!... So you see, we gotta reach that valley before the winter rains... We been prayin' to be showed the way... Mebbe you're our answer.

SANDY: *(with an eye on Prudence)* Makes you feel kinda NOBLE bein' an answer to a prayer, Travis...

TRAVIS: *(thoughtfully)* An' the Elder's offering a nice fair price for our hosses...

WIGGS: Fair! Why, I'll be go to...

PERKINS: Elder.

TRAVIS: But that's a mighty long, rough stretch o' country between here and the San Juan... and I'll be honest, Elder, I just don't think you can make it with wagons... No sir, you better count us out... Besides, my partner and me was figgerin' on settlin' a while and playin' a little high-low.

WIGGS: *(bitterly)* Gamblin' on a card game... and a hundred families gamblin' their lives on us!... Come on, Adam, we been wastin' time!

INTERIOR—MARSHAL'S OFFICE—DAWN

Sandy, Travis, the marshal, and three members of his posse have spent the night claiming low.

9

TRAVIS: *(taking the pot)* High, low, jack an' the game . . . I shot the moon!

> *He scoops in the chips as the Mormon bullhorn bre   He and Sandy look up inquiringly. One of the players shov   is chair back.*

FIRST PLAYER: Mormons stirrin' early . . .

> *He crosses to the door and peers off.*

> *At his statement Sandy and Travis exchange uncomfortable glances.*

FIRST PLAYER: Looks like they're gettin' ready to move out.

MARSHAL: *(sourly)* Blame fools! That ain't no country for wagons . . . Deal. *(ha 's cards to Travis)* An' if you claim low again, you better start runnin' . . .

> *As Travis deals, the bullhorn sounds again.*

EXTERIOR—MORMON CAMP—FULL SHOT—DAWN

The Mormon wagons are drawn up, ready for the move out. In front of them, standing in a rough semi-circle, are the members of the expedition. In addition to Wiggs and Perkins, there are about eight other men and fourteen or fifteen women and numerous children.

Among the Mormons who will figure prominently in the action are: Sister Ledyard, a stout matron with twinkling eyes and a zest for life that neither age nor lack of beauty can blunt. Sister Ledyard has outworn several husbands and is currently in the process of seeking another. She is an expert teamster, adept with the bullwhip and is the expedition's "bugler," her bugle being the bullhorn.

The Jamisons. He is a typical homesteader with a sweet-faced pregnant wife. They have a small daughter and a son, Billy, eight to ten years old. Billy, in turn, has a mongrel dog called Teddy.

Sam Jackson, a big, burly, Mormon farmer from Ohio. Unmarried but hoping to persuade Prudence to be his wife, Jackson has no love for Gentiles. He is personally brave, pugnacious, and jealous. His job is to ride guard on th rain wagon, which Sister Ledyard drives.

Among the others are Brother Schultz, a burly German blacksmith, and Brother Bolton, a tiny little man with two buxom wives and an alarmingly large family.

10

(Note: The Mormons are more Eastern than Western in their dress. None of them carry sidearms.)

Sister Ledyard lowers the bullhorn from her lips and Elder Wiggs takes a commanding position in front of the Mormons.

WIGGS: Brethren, it looks like we got a trial ahead of us, but it ain't the first time... We've gone it before alone... We're tough. We've had to be... ever since Brother Brigham led our people across the Plains... They survived and, dang it, so'll we... Now get to your wagons!

The Mormons move to their wagons. Sister Ledyard pauses beside the elder.

SISTER LEDYARD: *(confidently)* We'll get there, Elder... with the Lord's help!

WIGGS: *(not so confidently)* That's right, Sister Ledyard... But I was kinda wishin' those hoss-traders would lend Him a hand...

He indicates the bullhorn.

WIGGS: Sound it once more, Sister!

And as she brays her moose call.

INTERIOR—MARSHAL'S OFFICE—SANDY, TRAVIS, THE MARSHAL, AND PITCH PLAYERS

The quavering blast of the Mormon horn touches Travis and Sandy again.

TRAVIS: Claimin' low!

MARSHAL: *(flinging his hand in and rising)* That does it... C'mon... Time we was getting after them Cleggs anyway!

EXTERIOR—MARSHAL'S OFFICE

Saddled horses and pack animals carrying water kegs stand waiting. The posse mounts and rides off. Travis and Sandy stand watching. Then faintly comes the Mormon hymn, "All Is Well." The boys turn and stare.

FULL SHOT—FROM THEIR ANGLE—ON WAGON TRAIN

The Mormons, singing "All Is Well," as they move out. Women and children are in evidence in the passing wagons.

SANDY: *(concerned)* Gosh—all those women 'n children... What happens when they hit that desert?

11

TRAVIS: We warned 'em, didn't we?

He turns and starts for the corral, where their remuda is. Sandy, with many a backward look, slowly follows.

LONG SHOT—THE WAGON TRAIN—DAWN
The wagon train is moving steadily into the semi-arid country outside town.

FULL SHOT—CORRAL—DAWN
Sandy and Travis are saddling horses.

SANDY: *(wheedling)* And fifty a head's a good price, ain't it?

TRAVIS: *(stubbornly)* They's easier ways to make a livin'...

The boys mount, Sandy looks off again at the wagon train.

ANOTHER ANGLE—CORRAL, WITH BOYS IN FORE-GROUND, WAGON TRAIN IN DISTANT BACKGROUND—DAWN

SANDY: *(apprehensively)* Hey, they're not even goin' in the right direction!

Travis gives him a look of exasperation. He knows there is no alternative.

WIPE TO:

ANGLE ON HEAD OF COLUMN
Elder Wiggs is still driving the lead wagon as Sandy and Travis spur up alongside.

TRAVIS: Swing 'em west, Elder!

WIGGS: West? Why?

TRAVIS: The Lord forgot to provide any water where you're headin'...

WIGGS: *(happily)* I knowed you'd lend Him a hand, son!

Wiggs turns his team in the new direction. Travis takes up his position at the head of the column, just in front of the elder's lead horses.

TRAVIS: *(calling over his shoulder)* An' you owe me four hundred and fifty dollars.

WIGGS: *(happily)* Payable at the San Juan!

WIDER ANGLE

Showing the wagon train bending at it follows Wiggs's lead and takes up the new course. Travis rides in the lead and Sandy, guiding the remuda of horses, takes a position at the tail of the column.

WIPE TO:

LONG SHOT—LATE AFTERNOON

The wagon train is moving steadily across open country.
(Note: It is suggested that each successive shot of the wagons on the march should be of the train covering progressively more difficult terrain. The progression will be from rolling plain, to desert, to broken country torn by ravines, to foothills, and finally mountains.)
Sandy is riding well out in front, acting as point. Travis is riding close to the Perkins wagon, which is second in the file, following the Wiggs wagon.

ANOTHER ANGLE

As Sandy comes galloping back to the lead wagon, driven by Wiggs.

SANDY: *(calling to Wiggs)* Keep to the right of that mound.

Wiggs waves his understanding and Sandy continues to the Perkins wagon where Prudence sits beside her father. He reins in beside Travis.

SANDY: Rough up ahead . . . Better space 'em out.

Travis nods and wheels his horse, riding back to spread the word. Sandy rides closer to Prudence.

SANDY: You folks doin' all right?

PERKINS: *(a bit sourly)* We're all right.

Sam Jackson, who alone of the Mormons carries a rifle in his saddle holster, spurs jealously between the wagon and Sandy.

JACKSON: Anything I can do to make you more comfortable, Miss Prudence?

PRUDENCE: No, thank you kindly, Mister Jackson.

JACKSON: *(lamely but with a hostile glance at Sandy)* Well, if there is anything . . .

Sandy senses his antagonism and jealousy and, with an easy salute to the Perkins, spurs out ahead again.

PERKINS: *(staring stonily ahead)* Just you remember they're Gentiles! *Prudence flushes and looks swiftly at her father, then looks ahead again—making no answer. Sam Jackson nods his approval of this parental warning.*

JACKSON: *(to Perkins)* Strikes me Elder Wiggs is risking the Lord's wrath...hiring Gentiles to lead us.

PRUDENCE: *(flaring)* And strikes me Elder Wiggs knows more about such things than you do, Sam Jackson!

JACKSON: *(cajolingly)* No call to get riled, Miss Prudence...if you think it's seemly to be laughing and talking with Gentiles.

He spurs back down the line angrily, leaving an equally angry girl.

PERKINS: *(sourly)* Some girls would think twice before turning Brother Jackson away.

PRUDENCE: *(unimpressed)* Hum!

PERKINS: The Johnson sisters now...

PRUDENCE: *(angrily)* And no doubt he'll marry them both!

PERKINS: *(weakly defensive)* Now, daughter...sometimes a man gets a revelation...

PRUDENCE: *(not accepting it)* Any man of mine brought home a revelation I'd get a revelation of my own—the biggest stick I could lay my hand to!

PERKINS: *(sighing)* You sound just like your mother.

FULL SHOT—LATE AFTERNOON TOWARD DUSK—OPEN COUNTRY
The wagon train is nearing a creek, the stopping place for the night. The wagon drivers try to ease their teams down a slight incline bordering the creek bed.

ANOTHER ANGLE
Sandy gallops back to assist Mrs. Ledyard with the grain wagon. The bouncing of the wagon has forced her hat down over one eye and she struggles to push it back into place while handling her team.

FULL SHOT—WIGGS'S WAGON

Elder Wiggs is sawing on the reins of his team.

WIGGS: Easy, goldang ya! Easy, ya cussed, tarnation, iron-jawed ...!
He casts his eyes aloft.

WIGGS: Lord, whyn't you put some sense into these foul critters?
Travis spurs alongside.

TRAVIS: *(laughing)* Hang on, Elder!
He rides close to one of the lead horses and guides it down the slope to a stretch of level ground fringing in the stream. As the wagon moves along more easily, Travis drops back to ride alongside Wiggs.

MEDIUM CLOSE—MOVING—ON WIGGS AND TRAVIS

TRAVIS: *(grinning)* Could be I'm wrong, Elder ... But it sure sounded like you were usin' the words o' wrath back there!

WIGGS: *(quickly)* But I repented! Yessir, I tell you, son, there ain't a man in Utah quicker to lose his temper or quicker to repent than I am ... Lord and I we got an understandin' about that.
Travis laughs and spurs out front again.

LONG SHOT—DUSK

As the wagons slowly move along the bank of the stream toward a camping ground. They stop at Travis's signal, and we:

DISSOLVE

FULL SHOT—STREAM'S EDGE—TWILIGHT

Horses are being led to water. Passing Mormons carry firewood and buckets back to the encampment.

Prudence raises a brimming bucket from the stream and starts away with it, only to be intercepted by Sandy. He reaches for the bucket.

PRUDENCE: I can tote it.
Sandy takes the bucket.

SANDY: Sure you can, but there's no need to.
They turn and start up the slope when Sam Jackson plants himself squarely in Sandy's path and reaches aggressively for the bucket, snatching it away, jostling Sandy in the process.

JACKSON: *(during this) I'll* carry it.
> *Sandy recovers his balance and angrily takes a step forward. Jackson is obviously waiting for him to start swinging. But Travis's voice checks him.*

TRAVIS: Sandy!
> *Travis walks into the scene, seemingly unconscious of its tension. He plants his hand firmly on Sandy's shoulder.*

TRAVIS: Need a hand on the picket lines.
> *Sandy grudgingly turns away. Jackson shows his satisfaction and Prudence seems a little disappointed.*

MOVING SHOT—ON TRAVIS AND SANDY

TRAVIS: We got trouble enough without you stirrin' up more.

SANDY: Wasn't lookin' for trouble... But I ain't backin' down from it either.

TRAVIS: You wouldn't be much use with a busted arm... Besides...
> *With a backward glance.*

TRAVIS: ...looks to me like Miss Prudence can make up her own mind.
> *Sandy looks backward too.*

ANGLE ON PRUDENCE—FROM THEIR VIEWPOINT
She is toting her own bucket and Sam Jackson is disconsolately staring after her.

MEDIUM ON SANDY AND TRAVIS
Sandy grins and sets to work with a will, driving in the picket pins.

DISSOLVE

FULL SHOT—MORMON ENCAMPMENT NEAR STREAM—NIGHT
The Mormons are gathered around several small campfires, their wagons forming a backdrop behind them. Men are repairing broken harness, women are mending clothing or cradling their weary children in their arms.

16

ANOTHER ANGLE

As Sister Ledyard pauses in front of tiny little Brother Bolton.

SISTER LEDYARD: Evenin', Brother Bolton... How's the missus?

Two buxom women, who have been bending over some task behind Brother Bolton, simultaneously straightens up, turn to Sister Ledyard, with pleased smiles on their faces.

WOMEN: *(in unison)* Just fine, Sister!

ANOTHER ANGLE

Sandy stands leaning against a tree near the stream's edge, softly singing some romantic ballad—possibly "The Yellow Rose of Texas"—to the accompaniment of a guitar and accordion played by two of the Mormons.

(Note: Although the Mormons in general are interested in Sandy's song, it has special meaning to Prudence Perkins, who sits by herself and listens with rapt attention.)

FADE OUT

FADE IN

FULL SHOT—STREAM'S EDGE—DAY

It is early the next morning and the wagons are drawn up along the edge, ready to make the crossing. Horses are drinking and men and women are filling kegs and utensils with water.

Sandy canters down the line of wagons to pause at the Perkins wagon. Perkins and Prudence are dipping buckets into the stream.

SANDY: Better fill up some kettles, too, Miss Prudence... Fifty miles to the next water.

Sandy continues down the line of wagons, camera panning with him.

ANOTHER ANGLE

Mrs. Ledyard, on the driver's seat of the grain wagon, the center of attention. Elder Wiggs, sitting on his own wagon which is alongside hers, is looking at her as are Sam Jackson, Travis, and a few of the Mormon men.

17

MRS. LEDYARD: *(stubbornly)* I'm not budgin' an inch 'til I'm sure this grain won't get wet.

TRAVIS: *(resignedly)* Awright, Elder...you show her! Lead out!

Elder Wiggs whips up his horses and they start across the stream. The water doesn't reach above the hubs of his wheels. Travis, who has been in mid-stream, meets the Elder's team and guides it to the opposite bank.

MEDIUM CLOSE ON MRS. LEDYARD

Convinced, she nods her head and settles her hat firmly on her head.

MRS. LEDYARD: Now I'm satisfied!

She picks up her reins and the horses move out.

WIDER ANGLE ON STREAM CROSSING

As the grain wagon lurches out into the stream, to be followed in succession by the remaining wagons. Travis and Sandy are in the thick of the crossing, helping any rig that threatens to bog down...hauling lines, whipping stubborn beasts with their quirts to get the wagons in motion.

ANGLE ON PERKINS WAGON

As Sandy rides in, takes the bridle near the horse's mouth, and helps it ascend the far bank. He tips his hat jauntily to Prudence.

PRUDENCE: *(smiling after him)* Thank you, Mister Owens.

ANOTHER ANGLE

As Sandy spurs up beside Travis to help him and two Mormon boys drive the remuda horses through the stream.

As the last wagon passes, Travis looks off, grins and the camera pans him to young Billy Jamison, standing knee-deep in the stream, hauling on a huge bucket and vainly trying to overtake his parents' wagon. Near the boy is frisking a happy mongrel dog, Teddy. In the boy's pants band is stuck a huge old-fashioned .44 revolver. Travis rides closer.

TRAVIS: Catch up, bub!

He swings down and plucks the water bucket from the youngster's

18

hand and swings it almost in the same motion on the dropped tailgate of the Jamison wagon.
Billy grabs of hold the tailgate and swings himself aboard—wet to his hips. He pulls the revolver out and carefully wipes the barrel on his sleeve.

TRAVIS: Don't shoot me now.

Billy aims at the sky and snaps the trigger.

BILLY: Can't . . . no bullets.

Travis laughs and spurs on ahead, crossing the stream, racing to regain his place at the head of the column.

FULL SHOT—THE WAGON TRAIN

The stream behind it, it moves at a steady pace toward an arid wasteland stretching far ahead.

DISSOLVE

FULL SHOT—THE WAGON TRAIN—DESERT

It is several hours later. The wagons move at a slow crawl across an arid wasteland. A brassy sun beats with unrelenting intensity upon the trudging caravan. Mormon men and women walk beside their laboring teams. Only the smallest of the children are permitted to ride.
Travis, who is leading his horse, comes to a stop and looks off concernedly as the grain wagon comes into sight, its team being led by Mrs. Ledyard. She is dusty, disheveled, and at first glimpse seems near the point of exhaustion.

CLOSER ANGLE—MOVING

As Travis joins Mrs. Ledyard.

TRAVIS: Mebbe you oughta ride a bit, ma'am.

MRS. LEDYARD: Young man, I'll have you know I pushed a cart from Troy, New York, to Salt Lake thirty years ago—following Brigham Young.

Travis doffs his hat in a polite bow.

TRAVIS: *(drily)* I hope you caught him, ma'am!

Mrs. Ledyard is taken aback, and then she sees the humor.

19

MRS. LEDYARD: *(chuckling)* I tried... I tried!

ANOTHER ANGLE
Travis moves ahead.
Billy Jamison surreptitiously picks up his foot-weary dog and stows him away on the tailgate of the wagon. The boy signals Travis to keep his secret, placing his forefinger to his lips. Travis returns the signal and plods on up front beside Elder Wiggs.

ANGLE AT FRONT OF WAGON TRAIN—TRAVIS AND WIGGS
The Elder is moving ahead like a dogged little burro, with his eyes fixed on the horizon. He neither turns nor slackens his pace as Travis comes alongside.
TRAVIS: Care to take my horse... ride a while?
Wiggs barely deigns to look at him, tries to spit—but can only spit cotton.
WIGGS: Like to accommodate you, son, but a horse'd only slow me down...
After a moment he speaks again...
WIGGS: How far would you say we've come?
TRAVIS: Ten—twelve miles.
WIGGS: Then we got forty more miles o' desert.
TRAVIS: Yessir, and after that we come to...
WIGGS: *(busting in)* Don't want to hear about it... The Lord and I got enough on our minds just gettin' across this desert... We'll worry about the next part when we come to it.
Travis grins and continues on out front.

EXTERIOR—DESERT—SANDY AND TRAVIS—DAY
Sandy turns as Travis comes up. Sandy also is leading his horse. They pass a canteen, take cautious swallows.
SANDY: How they doing?
Travis merely shrugs noncommittally.
SANDY: Folks like them aren't made for this kind of country.
TRAVIS: There isn't *anybody* made for this kind of country... not even the Navajos.

Sandy looks around a little nervously.

SANDY: Yeah...and that *would* be something, wouldn't it!...

He faces Travis.

SANDY: Almost wish we hadn't agreed to do this, Travis.

He breaks off as the wind brings a sound like a distant drumming and a snatch of melody.

SANDY: It's a responsibility.

He frowns again, as the wind brings the drumming once more. Sandy looks perplexedly at Travis and sees that he, too, is frowning and staring off.

SANDY: It's...Say, do you hear anything?

Travis listens intently. A fresh gust of wind brings the sound of singing to them more clearly.

TRAVIS: *(puzzled)* Unless we're both loco, I do.

Both boys mount and ride off in the direction of the strange sounds. The camera holds on them as they ride off.

ANOTHER ANGLE—DESERT RAVINE—DAY

As Sandy and Travis complete their ride, pull up their horses, and gape at what they see. Now a recitative song is clearly heard to the accompaniment of a ragged beat of a bass drum and an occasional chord plucked on a guitar. Still staring, the boys swing off their horses and lead them slowly forward.

FULL SHOT—RAVINE—DAY

The sight presented amply accounts for the boys' bewilderment. There is, preeminently, a gaudy medicine wagon stranded in the ravine. Across its sides are the words:

DR. A. LOCKSLEY HALL

KICKAPOO SNAKE OIL

&

LIGHTNING ELIXIR

(and in somewhat smaller letters, to one side:)

Teeth   Hair

Pulled   Restored

Gathered around the wagon are four people: Hall, the medicine man; Mr. Peachtree, his roustabout and drumbeater; Florey, his long-time fiancée; and the gal called Denver.

Hall is the Eternal Ham, a charlatan, a poseur, but withal a Man of Distinction. His age is a few years on either side of 50. His frock coat and beaver hat are scarcely younger. He stands on a platform formed by the dropped tailgate of the wagon. He holds a bottle of his elixir in one hand, using it as a baton as he conducts his musicians.

Mr. Peachtree, his grizzled handyman and valet, wears a makeshift bandsman uniform with a drummer-boy cap. He also sits on the platform, presiding over a bass drum—a fixed smile on his face, his eyes glazed.

Florey—professionally Mlle. Fleurette Phyffe—occupies a droopy-seated wicker armchair. She holds a torn but dainty parasol over her head. She is a flouncy woman, still handsome and obviously once a stunner. She keeps a bottle of elixir close by and she is studying the professor with obvious admiration.

Denver is perched on a wardrobe trunk on the ground near the platform. She holds a guitar which she plucks in a rough accompaniment of the professor's recitation. She sits with one leg negligently crossed high above the knee. Denver is in her twenties— and most of her years have been tough ones.

The foursome at first pays no attention to the approach of the boys. Without water for three days and forced to drink their supply of patent medicine (86 proof), they have reached that stage of intoxication where nothing would strike them as being out of the ordinary.

The professor is delivering his recitative—(either a song or a verse to be decided upon later). Fleurette is the first to see the newcomers. She stands tipsily, crosses to the professor, and plucks vaguely at his elbow.

FLOREY: Gus—we've got an audience...

The professor turns and peers off in a direction several yards to the boys' right.

FLOREY: *(pointing with a waving finger)* Out front, Gus.

Hall swivels and tries to focus his eyes on the indicated point. He smiles vacantly, welcoming Travis and Sandy as they approach.

22

ANOTHER ANGLE
As the boys reach the foot of the improvised stage. Denver has eyes only for Travis.

SANDY: *(with uncertainty)* Howdy.

TRAVIS: *(equally puzzled)* Heard your music an'...

But he gets no farther, for the professor assumes the air of a master of ceremonies and claps his hands loudly.

HALL: *(clapping)* On stage, everybody! Mr. Peachtree!... strike up the band!

Mr. Peachtree beats a fanfare on a trapdrum. Then he picks up a banjo and starts a soft-shoe number as the professor and Florey go into a typical medicine-show routine of the period.

Sandy and Travis look at one another in bewilderment, then turn at the sound of Elder Wiggs's voice coming from off screen.

WIGGS'S VOICE: *(off screen)* Well, I'll be go to...

REVERSE ANGLE
Wiggs has come to a shocked standstill, backed by the advance guard of Mormons, including Sam Jackson and Adam Perkins.

WIGGS: By thunder! It's a hootchy-kootchy show!

The Mormons start to advance toward the medicine wagon.

A NEW ANGLE
Sandy picks up a half-empty bottle of elixir standing on the edge of the platform. He samples its contents and spits out a mouthful.

SANDY: Wow!

The professor and Florey continue, meanwhile, with their pathetic attempt at a dance routine.

ANOTHER ANGLE
Featuring Denver, as she rises, letting the guitar fall to the ground unnoticed. She takes a cigarette from the front of her dress and walks unsteadily but purposefully toward Travis, looking to neither right or left. When she is a yard away, she pauses, swaying on her feet.

DENVER: Got a match?

She puts the cigarette between her lips and waits expectantly, her eyes never leaving Travis. He takes a wooden match, strikes it and the girl puffs. She chokes and flings the cigarette away.

DENVER: *(unsteadily)* You might ... offer ... a lady ... a drink.

Travis looks at Sandy and the bottle of elixir. Sandy hesitates and then offers it to the girl. Denver, with a loose, uncontrolled motion of her arm, knocks the bottle aside.

DENVER: Not that stuff ... That's all we've had for three days ... Water ... Just a drink of water ...

With that her knees suddenly let go and she slumps to the ground at Travis's feet. Travis drops to one knee beside her and cradles her head as Hall and Florey come to the end of their routine and stand at the edge of the stage, groggily awaiting applause. The Mormons come closer in the background, still staring speechless at the spectacle. Sandy looks from the girl to the bottle in his hand.

SANDY: *(awed tones)* Golly! No wonder! Three days with nothin' to drink but ...

He winces.

SANDY: Dr. Hall's Lightning Elixir!

At this point Hall, who has only caught the last words spoken by Sandy, takes a theatrical stance and begins his spiel.

HALL: *(with gestures)* Yes, friends! Guaranteed to cure every ailment known to man or beast ... from female complaints to bog spavin!

He suddenly gasps and reels back against the side of the wagon. He is in danger of falling, but Wiggs jumps up on the stage and supports him.

WIGGS: Easy, brother ...

In tones of sharp command.

WIGGS: Sam ... Bring me some water! Fast!

DISSOLVE

FULL SHOT—DESERT RAVINE—DAY

A knot of Mormons is standing some distance from the medicine wagon as Wiggs makes his report. Sandy and Travis stand near him, as does Peachtree—from whom (we may assume) Wiggs has obtained most of his information. Peachtree nods or shakes his head, rather proud of it all, as Wiggs explains.

WIGGS:... so with their water gone, Mister Peachtree here poured two quarts of Lightning Elixir into a bucket and gave it to the mule...

Peachtree practically takes a bow.

WIGGS: Last they see of her, she was goin' over the hill like a Kansas twister... And here they been ever since... Question is, what we goin' to do?

JACKSON: *(grudgingly)* Give 'em a team, I guess, 'n enough water to get 'em to Crystal City.

Peachtree seems alarmed—and taps the elder's arm.

WIGGS: *(uncomfortably)* Well, now, from what Mister Peachtree says—the professor wasn't exactly popular in Crystal City... That's where they come from.

JACKSON: *(bluntly)* You mean they were run out?

WIGGS: *(amending it)* Invited out... So they started off for California.

MRS. LEDYARD: Poor man! Bein' driven out like that with his wife an' daughter!

Peachtree gapes and shakes his head negatively.

WIGGS: Ain't quite that way, Sister Ledyard... Miss Denver—that's the young one—ain't his daughter and Miss Fleurette—fine figger of a woman too—she ain't exactly...

JACKSON: *(angrily)* That cuts it! We give 'em what they need and get along.

Travis straightens and takes a step forward.

TRAVIS: *(evenly)* I don't believe these people are up to travelin' alone, Mister Jackson.

JACKSON: *(sourly)* They will be—when they're sober.

TRAVIS: We'll pick up the California trail in two-three days.

Jackson shakes his head stubbornly.

PERKINS: Don't think we ought to take up with their kind of people, Elder.

Travis grows a trifle angry.

TRAVIS: *(angrily)* I'm not leavin' 'em... That's flat.

JACKSON: *(flaring)* You hired out to us...

Wiggs, to prevent trouble, interrupts.

WIGGS: Hold on there! Calm down! Now I ain't so sure the Lord didn't put 'em in our path for a reason.

The Mormons listen attentively. Wiggs continues in a quietly persuasive voice.

WIGGS: As I see it, He ain't one to waste His energy ... an' He sure went to a lot of trouble gettin' these people into this fix.

Now his manner becomes stern, almost Jehovah-like.

WIGGS: And if I was HIM, I wouldn't want anybody messin' up MY plans!

His words have their effect. The Mormons shift uncomfortably. Sandy and Travis exchange glances—amused at the elder's ability to get his own way.

PERKINS: *(surrendering)* Well ... putting it that way!

BROTHER BOLTON: *(calling off)* Ezra, hitch up a team here!

One of the stripling boys runs to do his bidding and Wiggs again faces the assembly.

WIGGS: Who'll volunteer to drive?

No one advances, fearful of their neighbor's opinion, unwilling to risk contamination.

WIGGS: Brother Schultz, how about that oldest boy of yours?

Schultz shakes his head, but from behind the men, Prudence pushes forward and steps into the vacant area between Wiggs and the Mormons. They look at her in shocked silence.

PRUDENCE: I'll drive their wagons, Elder.

WIGGS: *(pleased with her)* All right, folks, back to your wagons! We've wasted enough time.

ANGLE ON MEDICINE WAGON

Sandy comes forward to assist Prudence into the driver's seat. Travis stands near.

SANDY: This is right Christian of you, ma'am!

As she climbs aboard, Wiggs crosses to Travis.

WIGGS: Let's get moving, boy!

TRAVIS: *(calling off)* Catch up!

He looks at Wiggs with a twinkle in his eyes.

TRAVIS: You and Lord think a lot alike, don't you, Elder?

Wiggs's mouth jerks as he conceals a smile.

WIGGS: Not always, son ... Sometimes He takes a little persuadin'.

DISSOLVE

26

LONG SHOT—THE WAGON TRAIN—DESERT—SUNSET

The train moves slowly into the setting sun, with the medicine wagon now a strange part of the caravan. As the wagon continues, the sky seems to darken—suggesting the coming of night.

FADE OUT

FADE IN

CLOSE SHOT—SISTER LEDYARD—DESERT—DAY

As she sounds reveille on the Mormon bullhorn. The ear-splitting blast is enough to awaken the dead. As Mrs. Ledyard takes the bullhorn from her lips, someone starts beating on a tin dish basin, and in the background we see Mormon families tumbling sleepily from their wagons.

ANGLE ON PICKET LINES

Under the watchful supervision of Sandy and Travis, water is being poured from kegs into a row of buckets which the Mormons are setting forth in front of the horses. The water is carefully doled out, with not a drop being spilled. The men look on thirstily as the animals lower their muzzles into the water.

ANOTHER ANGLE

Favoring Sandy and Travis—with Sam Jackson watering a horse in the near background.

Sandy squints aloft at the brassy sky, his eyes crinkling at the glare, and he eases his hat back to wipe the sweat from his forehead.

SANDY: Be hotter'n hell by noon.

Jackson glares at him and comes closer, aggressively.

JACKSON: Mind your language!

SANDY: I wasn't cussin'.

JACKSON: Said "hell."

SANDY: "Hell" ain't cussin'... It's ... it's ... geography ... A name of a place, like you might say Abilene, or Salt Lake City.

JACKSON: *(still angrier)* Don't you go makin' any remarks about Salt Lake City!

27

Sandy gives him a look of disgust, but with effort curbs his temper and moves away. Jackson looks after him triumphantly. As Sandy passes Travis, the Texan pats him on the shoulder.

ANGLE ON MEDICINE WAGON—DESERT—DAY
Locksley Hall rounds the side of the medicine wagon in a partly dressed state, followed by his faithful servitor, Peachtree. The professor lacks a shirt, but wears a "dickey" and his suspenders are draped over his bare shoulders. Peachtree is carefully brushing his beaver hat.

Hall winces and glares off as the bullhorn blasts another call.

HALL: Great Scott! What is that braying?

PEACHTREE: Mess call.

HALL: *(regally)* Have it stopped!

Peachtree nods and obediently starts away as the professor sets up a small mirror on the side of the wagon. A water bucket stands on an up-ended box—with brush, razor already set out for him.

FULL SHOT—MRS. LEDYARD
Winding the bullhorn as Peachtree approaches. She gives him a bright smile, and bears down on him like a ship under sail.

MRS. LEDYARD: *(heartily)* Well, if it ain't a fellow musician!... Mornin', brother! Had your breakfast yet?

Peachtree shakes his head timidly. Mrs. Ledyard grabs his arm.

MRS. LEDYARD: Well, you come right along. Nothin' pleasures me more than watchin' a man each his vittles! You married, brother?

Peachtree shakes his head—this time with real apprehension. Mrs. Ledyard's grip tightens. She starts to lead him off.

MRS. LEDYARD: Well, now ain't that a coincidence! Neither am I!...

Peachtree wriggles free and beats a retreat. She looks after him with dismay.

ANGLE ON MEDICINE WAGON
Hall dips his shaving brush in the water bucket and starts to work up a lather with a piece of soap as Florey climbs down from the wagon with his shirt in her hands, biting off a piece of thread close to one of the buttons.

FLOREY: Here's your shirt, Gus.

Hall stiffens.

HALL: *(regally)* The name is not Gus!... I am known, have been known, as A. Locksley Hall... I have even won some small fame under that cognomen!... Please remember that, Miss Phyffe!

FLOREY: *(patiently)* Yes, Gus... Here's your shirt... I got the buttons from Mrs. Schultz... She took them off her husband's pants. My, they're nice!

Hall, who has been on the verge of dipping the soapy brush into the bucket, freezes and gapes at her.

HALL: Her husband's pants?

FLOREY: No, Gus... The Schultzes... and the Jamisons... all of them...

She sighs wistfully.

FLOREY:... real nice folks.

HALL: Nice? Did you ever play Salt Lake City?

Florey shakes her head.

HALL: A theatrical Siberia!... They would stone Will Shakespeare himself!

FLOREY: *(placatingly)* It's only a few days, Gus... Please try to get along...

Hall is about to dip his lathered brush into the bucket, when Travis's voice arrests him.

TRAVIS: Excuse me, Professor...

Travis comes from behind the professor and checks the brush's descent.

TRAVIS:... but shavin' ain't permitted... we're kinda low on water.

HALL: *(exasperated but patient)* Young man, I have never—in all my years of trouping—appeared before my public unshaven... I have no intention of doing so now.

He extends the brush again, but Travis deftly takes the bucket and passes it to Sandy, who has joined them.

TRAVIS: I'm real sorry...

He turns to go and is almost deluged by a basin of water emptied at his feet. It has been tossed from the back of the wagon by Denver, whose bare arm now waves the basin.

DENVER'S VOICE: *(from within the wagon)* Will you rinse this, Florey?

Travis takes the basin from her hand.

TRAVIS: Shouldn't have done that, ma'am.

Denver pokes her head out the wagon bow.

DENVER: Shouldn't have done what?

TRAVIS: Taken a wash out here in the desert . . . We need that water for horses.

Denver leans out a little, revealing bare shoulders.

DENVER: *(sweetly)* I'm sorry . . . I won't take another bath until you tell me to.

Travis—and Sandy—have been studying the bare shoulders with mounting embarrassment.

TRAVIS: Yes'm, I will . . . I mean . . . well, that is . . .

He backs away.

TRAVIS: You folks better hitch up!

And he and Sandy back off and hurry away. Denver looks after him with amusement and parts the canvas bows, revealing that she has been fully dressed but with her blouse pulled low off her shoulders. She jumps down and adjusts her blouse and looks off after Travis, laughing at him.

Sam Jackson comes up, leading their team of horses.

JACKSON: *(sourly)* Time to catch up!

HALL: Young man! I don't suppose you'd undertake to harness the beasts for me . . . No, I see that you wouldn't.

JACKSON: You'll do your share of the work, mister . . . and that goes for your women, too.

Jackson stalks off and Hall glares after him.

HALL: *(sarcastically)* Nice folks!

FULL SHOT—TRAVIS AND SANDY—DESERT—DAY

They sit their horses at the head of the assembling wagon train.

TRAVIS: *(calling)* Catch up and lead out!

He and Sandy walk their horses out onto the reaching desert.

DISSOLVE

LONG SHOT—WAGON TRAIN—DESERT—DAY

Sandy's prediction about the heat is borne out. The sun beats down

30

unmercifully on the weary Mormons. The wagons crawl along in parallel columns—with men and women leading the exhausted teams.

Out front Sandy and Travis trudge stolidly beside their mounts. Travis pauses and waits for the wagons to come up.

ANOTHER ANGLE—WAGON TRAIN

As Travis stands, watching his charges, we see that the Mormons are having a rough time. Men and women pass him without a side glance, their eyes focused on a distant objective, all their efforts devoted to the task of setting one foot in front of another.

The Jamisons pass—with Mr. Jamison steadying his wife with an arm about her waist. Young Billy trails along, one hand grasping a dangling chain from the rear of the wagon so that it helps pull him along.

Another wagon—the Bolton wagon—rocks along. A group of children huddle on the tailgate, not speaking—numbed by the heat and the monotony of the trek. One of the mothers cradles a baby in her arms, fans it to create some illusion of stirring air.

There is a sudden commotion as one of the horses of the medicine wagon begins to plunge and rear.

Florey is driving, with the professor walking near the horses' heads and Denver and Peachtree stumbling alongside. Hall manfully tries to pull the horse down, but Travis finally succeeds in pulling him under control.

TRAVIS: Wants water! Fetch me a cloth and bucket!

Peachtree comes up with a pail. Travis dips a cloth in it and sponges the horse's nostrils.

TRAVIS: *(to Peachtree)* Same for the other one.

He passes the cloth to Peachtree and turns to study Denver.

MEDIUM CLOSE—ANGLE ON MEDICINE WAGON— DESERT—DAY

Denver has been having a tough time. Her disordered hair and streaked face attest to it. But she isn't complaining. She leans against the wagon and, indifferent to a show of leg, slips off one high-heeled slipper and dumps a cupful of sand from it. Travis notes this with some concern, crosses to her and takes the slipper.

31

TRAVIS: *(incredulously)* You been walkin' in these? Haven't you anything more ... more ...?

DENVER: No.

Without a word, Travis starts off—still holding her slipper. Denver takes a limping step after him.

DENVER: Hey!

But Travis ignores her, mounts and rides off toward the Perkins wagon.

LONG SHOT—FROM DENVER'S ANGLE

As Travis rides in to the Perkins wagon and conducts a brief pantomime with Prudence—showing her the slipper, pointing back to Denver—clearly explaining the girl's predicament. Prudence leans into the wagon and produces a pair of shoes. Travis tips his hat and comes back.

ANOTHER ANGLE—TRAVIS AND DENVER

Travis dismounts and offers her a pair of stout, sensible walking shoes.

TRAVIS: Here, try these on!

He up-ends one of the empty water buckets for her to sit on. She slips on one shoe, then the other. During this:

TRAVIS: Hope they ain't too big.

DENVER: She your wife?

TRAVIS: Miss Prudence? ... No, ma'am ... How they feel?

Denver stands—a little surprised and possibly a little annoyed—to find that Prudence has as dainty a foot as she.

DENVER: Fine ... *(second thought)* A little large, maybe, but ... thanks. *(grudgingly)* And thank your lady friend too.

TRAVIS: She ain't that either.

He starts for his horse and leads it ahead.

TRAVIS: *(calling)* Catch up!

As he rides out, Denver looks after him—a little reflectively, touched by his kindness.

ANOTHER ANGLE

Including Florey on wagon seat.

FLOREY: Now that was real sweet . . . looks like you got yourself a beau, Denver.

Denver's face hardens to its usual hard, half-contemptuous mask.
DENVER: That rube? . . . No, thanks!

The wagon pulls out and Denver resumes her walk. She notices she still is holding one of the small, flimsy slippers. With a shrug, she tosses it over her shoulder and strides on.

DISSOLVE

FULL SHOT—DESERT—LATE AFTERNOON
The train moves so slowly as to seem almost at a standstill. Behind it, stretching for miles, are the marks of its progress.
Then, over a hillock of sand and scrub, ride Sandy and Travis. They wave their hats in encouragement.
SANDY—TRAVIS: *(calling)* Water! Water!

SERIES OF SHOTS—STAMPEDE
1.   *Men and women come to a stumbling stop at Travis's cry. They look up with disbelief, then with wild hope. Through dry and dust-caked lips they mouth the one word "water"— croaking it out.*
2.   *Horses plunge, with rolling eyes and flaring nostrils, as they catch the water scent and drivers run close and try to pull the frantic beasts to a halt.*
3.   *Travis and Sandy ride among the plunging teams, calling to their drivers.*
SANDY—TRAVIS: Hang onto 'em! Hold 'em in! Don't let 'em run!
4.   *Angle on wagons as Mormon men clamber aboard and haul back on the reins as some of the teams break into a lunging gallop toward the distant water.*
5.   *Close on one wagon with a cargo of terrified children as the team starts to run away. Its driver is caught off balance as it starts and is hurled to the ground. He gets to his feet and starts running helplessly after it as the wagon goes careening off. But Travis has seen the runaway, spurs after it and, in a daring exhibition of horsemanship, pulls the team to a walk.*

33

6.   *Reverse angle, from across the stream, as the wagons breast the rise and plunge down the gentle slope to the water's edge. The horses do not stop until the wagons are hub-deep in the stream. Then men, women, and children fling themselves headlong, lapping the water a few inches from the muzzles of their horses.*

FADE OUT

FADE IN

FULL SHOT MORMON ENCAMPMENT—RIVER'S EDGE—NIGHT

Their weariness forgotten, the Mormons are celebrating the desert crossing with a lively hoedown. The tailgate of the medicine wagon has been lowered to form a platform for the musicians and the caller—Travis. A few lengths of tarpaulin have been pegged out on the hard-packed ground to form the dance floor.

Guitar, fiddle, banjo, and accordion provide the music, with Peachtree tapping time as he plays the fiddle. Travis is calling the turns for "The Texas Star."

Behind the musicians and a little to one side are the medicine show people, who remain aloof from the dancing.

Elder Wiggs is prominent among the dancers.

Sandy and Prudence are partners.

Mrs. Ledyard, at one point, swings away from her partner, grabs hold of Mr. Peachtree and jerks him from the platform. Peachtree flips his fiddle to an onlooker who catches it and joins in the playing, scarcely missing a beat.

As the music ends and the dancers start from the floor:

ANOTHER ANGLE—NEAR MEDICINE WAGON

The professor, Florey, and Denver have been watching the scene. Florey's eyes are bright. Denver—a cigarette in her lips—watches the dancers leave the floor with amused indifference. She smiles mockingly as Elder Wiggs approaches, mopping his forehead. His genial expression alters at the sight of Denver's cigarette.

DENVER: *(mockingly)* Hi, Elder!... You cut a mean allemande-left for a man your age.

WIGGS: *(sharply)* An' I'll cut a meaner hickory switch for you, young woman, if you don't take that cigareet out o' your mouth!

Denver merely laughs and blows out a puff of smoke. Wiggs takes a threatening step closer.

WIGGS: I mean it!

Denver is a little surprised, then laughs.

DENVER: Why, I believe you do!

Nevertheless she tosses the cigarette away.

DENVER: That better?

WIGGS: *(grudgingly)* Some... Now if you'd wipe that raspberry smear off your lips mebbe I'd tell some of the brethren to dance with you.

DENVER: *(with a touch of patronage)* You Mormons don't drink, you don't smoke, you don't gamble... How is it you haven't outlawed dancing?

Wiggs looks her straight in the eye, but without anger.

WIGGS: We don't drink or smoke because we don't need stimulants...we don't gamble because we believe in *working* for what we get... But singin' and dancing?... Well, there's more o' that in heaven than in the other place.

His words impress Denver and the professor in spite of themselves and they clearly convince Florey.

FLOREY: *(wistfully)* I haven't danced in...when was it, Gus?

WIGGS: Then high time you did!

And he grabs her hand and leads her to the dance area—with the professor and Denver looking after them in surprise, and in the professor's case, with a little touch of jealousy.

ANGLE ON DANCE AREA

As Wiggs leads Florey out. Several of the Mormon couples look at him askance—surprised to see him with a scarlet woman. Travis, standing on the platform, notices the Mormons' attitude. He sees that Sandy is standing alone, since Sam Jackson has claimed Prudence as his partner.

TRAVIS: *(to Sandy)* Your turn, Sandy... Call this'n!

As he jumps down from the platform, Sandy takes his place. The

35

camera pans Travis as he walks toward Denver. Meanwhile Sandy is assembling the squares.

SANDY: *(off screen)* Choose your partners, form your squares . . . Gents on this side, ladies on theirs . . .

CLOSER ANGLE—NEAR MEDICINE WAGON

Travis comes up to Denver.

TRAVIS: *(formal bow)* May I have the pleasure, ma'am?

Denver hesitates and the professor shoots her a warning glance, but Denver juts her chin stubbornly.

DENVER: Why not?

And she swishes out onto the floor with Travis.

ANGLE ON DANCE FLOOR

Again there should be the suggestion of Mormon tension and hostility toward the medicine show people as Travis and Denver take their places in a square with Sam Jackson and Prudence. Only Prudence smiles a welcome to Denver. But the music strikes up and Sandy begins to call some dance on the order of "Sally Goodin" or "The Old Pine Tree."

The dance progresses with increasing friendliness on the part of all. Florey's obvious delight wins over her partners. Denver, in another square, passes from hand to hand and her own defiant manner undergoes a change until she is laughing as light-heartedly as the rest.

But as the dance reaches its peak, the music falters and Sandy ceases his calling. The dancers turn toward the platform in some surprise, only to see the musicians staring off over their heads at something on the edge of the campfires. As they turn, they too gape.

ANOTHER ANGLE—WHAT THEY SEE

From the outer darkness into the circle of light step four men—the Cleggs. Jesse holds his shotgun, Reese his rifle at the ready. Uncle Shiloh is a little in the lead, his left arm in an improvised sling. The four men look spent and exhausted—and because of that are more deadly than usual.

The unspoken menace of the Cleggs is so evident that the Mormons

36

back away, the men putting the women a little behind them, and they form a defensive semi-circle as the Cleggs slowly come into the full light of the cleared dance area. Sandy quietly takes a stand near Travis.

SHILOH: *(tentatively)* Evenin'...

No one replies or makes a move. Shiloh's eyes rove left and right; then he singles out Wiggs as the head of the group and he speaks almost directly to him.

SHILOH: Me an' the boys seen your fires. Scared at first you might be Navajo. Then I heard your hoedown. Said to Floyd here, wherever there's singin' an' dancin' you can be sure there's Christian folks. Never did know a bad man had any music in him ... Thought maybe you'd help out some strangers down on their luck, maybe stake us for a feed?

He pauses and waits for an answer. For all his wheedling, whining words, there is a deadly threat behind them. Wiggs takes a step closer to Shiloh.

WIGGS: You're welcome to share the little we've got.

The Cleggs relax a little. Shiloh smiles crookedly as he turns to his boys.

SHILOH: That's neighborly, mister ... real neighborly ... Hear that, boys? These good God-fearin' folks is biddin' us welcome!

ANOTHER ANGLE—MOVING

Wiggs turns and leads the way toward the stew-pots near the wagons. Shiloh, thumb hooked in his gun belt, follows him— trailed and flanked by Reese, then Floyd and Jesse. Shiloh resumes his glib, lying explanation.

SHILOH: We-uns been out huntin'... but had nothin' but hard scrabble ... pack hosses stompeded with all our grub, an' I fell 'n bust my shoulder.

Reese has paused at the sight of Denver, standing near Travis. Suddenly he pulls her to him and tries to kiss her. Travis moves to intervene, but Shiloh is quicker. As though he had eyes in the back of his head, he turns and brings his quirt across Reese's neck. He releases the girl.

Shiloh grins an apology to Denver.

SHILOH: Don't mind Reese ... He jist ain't seen a pretty gal in quite a spell ... Let's eat, Reese!

And rubbing his neck, Reese follows obediently as Shiloh resumes his course with Wiggs and, as though there had been no interruption, continues his lying explanation.

SHILOH: Shoulder's been hurtin' bad ... can't hardly sit my horse no more ...

Wiggs has led the way to the stew-pot. The four Cleggs crowd around and dig in hugely, but keeping their guns handy and their eyes on the Mormons. It is clear they have not been eating regularly.

CLEGGS: *(generally)* Smells good ... Don't pig it, Reese!

ANOTHER ANGLE

As Sandy draws close to Travis and Denver.

SANDY: *(softly, with apprehension)* You know who they are, don't you?

TRAVIS: *(nodding)* I know.

SANDY: What are we going to do?

JESSE'S VOICE: Hey, there!

Sandy and Travis start slightly—and look off.

ANOTHER ANGLE—PAST SANDY AND TRAVIS, TOWARD THE CLEGGS

Jesse is hunkered down on the ground with a plate of food in front of him, his shotgun in the crook of his arm, but obviously pointed at them.

JESSE: You two! What you whisperin' about?

Sandy and Travis make no reply.

JESSE: Got anything to say, say it out!

Still no reply.

JESSE: Come over here!

Sandy and Travis start toward him, walking gingerly—not knowing whether they are going to be shot in the belly.

ANOTHER ANGLE—THE CLEGG GROUP, SANDY AND TRAVIS, WIGGS

The Cleggs are all looking sharply and with suspicion at the two.

JESSE: They're the only ones totin' guns, Uncle Shiloh.

WIGGS: They're our wagonmasters.

Floyd slowly gets to his feet, his thumbs hooked casually in his gun belt, his feet braced apart—readiness in every inch as he confronts the two boys. He glances first at Sandy.

FLOYD: Ever draw on a man?

Sandy gulps, but shakes his head. Floyd's gaze shifts to Travis.

TRAVIS: *(quietly)* No, sir ... *(as an afterthought)* ... just snakes.

Floyd's eyes narrow slightly.

FLOYD: *(to Travis)* Mind if I heft your gun?

There is a moment of suspense. Then Travis slowly puts his hand on his gun butt. Floyd tenses slightly. And Jesse, whose shotgun never has left the boys, slides a finger closer to the trigger. Travis slowly draws the gun, then hands it butt first to Floyd. He hefts it.

FLOYD: Good balance.

Then he spins and, seemingly without an aim, fires at a billet of wood lying on the ground some distance away. The billet jumps. He fires again—splitting the billet in two.

Sandy looks bug-eyed at the demonstration. Only Travis seems strangely unimpressed.

Floyd complacently blows smoke out of the barrel and hands the gun back to Travis, who holsters it.

Jesse laughs but pats his shotgun.

JESSE: I like a shotgun better. Shoots wider.

Wiggs hasn't liked any of it, and the sooner he can rid the camp of these men, the better. He deliberately takes out a huge turnip of a silver watch and pointedly consults it.

WIGGS: Time we were turnin' in. Got a long day ahead ...

He faces the Cleggs.

WIGGS: So if you men'll just stack your plates over there when you're finished, we'll see you again sometime ...

SHILOH: *(easily)* Don't you worry about us ... We'll just set here 'n enjoy your fire for a while.

Wiggs's mouth tightens angrily, but he has no alternative.

WIGGS: Travis—you and Sandy better check the picket lines ...

FULL SHOT—MORMON CAMP

As Sandy and Travis start away and Wiggs rejoins his waiting group of Mormons.

WIGGS: *(calling)* Sound taps, Sister Ledyard.

The Mormons start to drift for their wagons—a little worriedly, glancing apprehensively at the Cleggs as they go. Sam Jackson checks Wiggs in the foreground.

JACKSON: I'm not turning in till they're gone.

WIGGS: *(sharply)* You'll obey orders.

Sister Ledyard lets loose her blast with the bullhorn and the Mormons disappear into their wagons. The professor, Denver, and Florey start for the medicine wagon.

Reese moves out into the emptying clearing and watches hungrily as Florey and then Denver climb into the wagon. He then strolls toward the professor, who is standing near.

ANGLE ON MEDICINE WAGON

Reese comes up to Hall, his eye still on the wagon.

RESSE: You her paw?

HALL: *(with dignity)* To the best of my knowledge, no!

REESE: Husband?

HALL: I have no conjugal ties.

REESE: *(suspiciously)* What's them?

HALL: Reduced to monosyllables, it means . . . NO!

REESE: You a preacher?

Hall has grown weary of this. Looking down his nose, he gestures grandly toward the lettering on the medicine wagon.

HALL: There I am, sir! . . . Read it at your leisure . . . And now, may I bid you good night.

He starts to turn away, but Reese catches his arm in a grip that leaves bruises.

REESE: I don't read so good . . . what's it say?

HALL: *(spelling out the words)* Doctor A. Locksley Hall . . . Kickapoo Snake Oil and Lightning Elixir . . . and in the small letters, Teeth Pulled, Hair Restored.

He is unprepared for Reese's reaction. With an amazed and exultant expression, the oaf grabs his arm still tighter and starts

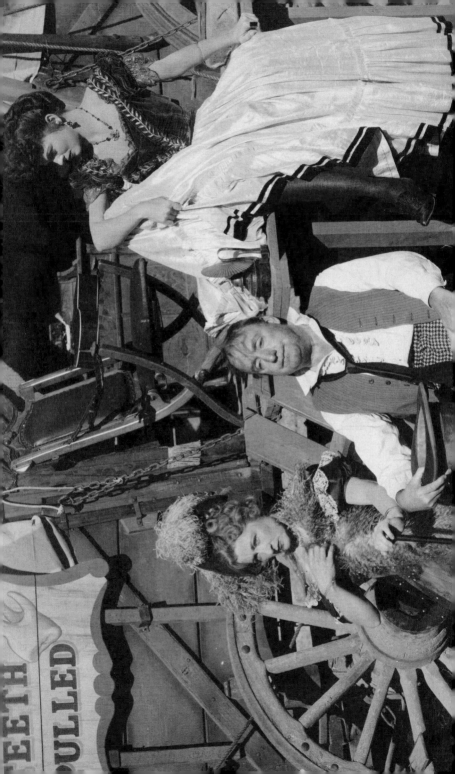

*pulling him—as he would a rag doll—away from the wagon and
toward the Clegg group, at the same time yelling the news.*

REESE: Uncle Shiloh...look yere what I found—a doctor!

ANOTHER ANGLE—CLEGG GROUP

Shiloh looks up eagerly as Hall is pushed close.

SHILOH: A doctor! Well, now that's real providential... Be obliged if
you'd take a look at my shoulder, Doc.

HALL: *(uncomfortably)* Well...I am not certain, sir...

Floyd comes aggressively closer.

FLOYD: Fix his shoulder!

*Hall surrenders. He gets to one knee beside Shiloh and slips back
the outlaw's shirt. Wiggs has returned to the group and looks on.
Hall looks up with sudden alarm.*

HALL: You've been shot! That's a bullet wound!

*Reese giggles at the professor's astonishment over anything so
commonplace.*

SHILOH: *(grimly)* That's right... an' that chunk o'lead's still in there. Git
it out!

Hall gets to his feet.

HALL: I can't...I...I'm not qualified.

The Cleggs (Floyd, Jesse, and Reese) crowd him menacingly.

REESE: Said you was a doctor.

HALL: Figuratively, perhaps...but this is out of my line...

REESE: *(stubbornly)* Said you pull teeth.

FLOYD: Don't like liars.

His hands move suggestively to his guns.

FLOYD: Soon kill a liar as look at him... Said you was a doctor... If
you are, get busy...if you lied...

HALL: *(hastily)* I'll get my bag!

*He leaves, almost on the run. Sandy and Travis rejoin the group.
Shiloh looks up with a disarming smile.*

SHILOH: *(the fond parent)* One thing I taught my boys was never to
lie...Steal if you has to, an' kill if you must...but don't never
lie...That's the rule among us Cleggs...

WIGGS: *(sharply)* Did you say "Cleggs"... The *Cleggs* who murdered
that Wells-Fargo clerk back in Crystal City?

FLOYD: *(proudly)* Yeah—that's who we are.

SHILOH: *(overriding and silencing Floyd with a hand movement)* Murder's a hard word ... seein' as he shot first.

WIGGS: *(sternly)* I'm giving you thirty seconds to clear out of our camp!
> *His eyes lock with Shiloh's. Floyd and Jesse step back, to give themselves room to fire. Sandy and Travis wait. They are covered by Jesse's shotgun.*

SHILOH: *(measuring Wiggs for a coffin)* Thirty seconds ain't much time ... is it, Jesse? But if'n that's all he's givin' us ...
> *Travis knows that Shiloh is about to give the order for the execution. Quietly and with a disarming smile, he interposes himself between Wiggs and Jesse's shotgun.*

TRAVIS: No call to get excited, Elder ... Mister Clegg ain't askin' for much ... just to get that bullet out! ... Why, you'd do that for a mangy dog!
> *If he is insulting the Cleggs by this, it doesn't pointedly show—and the Cleggs, though suspicious, don't take up the point.*

TRAVIS: *(easily)* And famous outlaws like the Cleggs here ain't goin' to be wastin' their time with a peaceful wagon train o' Mormon farmers ... You got nothin' they want! ... Ain't that right, Mister Clegg?
> *Hall reappears, with a small sachel of crude knives and probes, and two large bottles of his elixir.*

SHILOH: It's the gospel truth, boy.

TRAVIS: *(drawing Wiggs away—and speaking to Hall)* Then—go ahead, Doc ...
> *The tension is eased, although both Reese and Jesse seem disappointed at the outcome. Hall nervously kneels beside Shiloh and uncorks a bottle of elixir.*

HALL: Drink this!
> *Shiloh smells it suspiciously.*

HALL: It's mostly alcohol ...
> *He looks nervously at Wiggs.*

HALL: ... with a little licorice for flavor.
> *Shiloh drinks deep.*

WIGGS: *(reproachfully, to Hall)* You got a lot to repent, Professor.
> *Shiloh doesn't like the licorice added to his likker.*

SHILOH: Sure have!

But he swallows again. Hall has taken out a knife and bends in on Shiloh.

HALL: You ready?

SHILOH: Hold on a minute!

He tilts the bottle back until its contents are gone. His eyes are a little glassy.

SHILOH: Get on with it...

And Hall leans in to make the first cut.

SAME SCENE—AN HOUR LATER

Hall is standing, rolling down his sleeves. Shiloh leans weakly back, propped against a wheel or blanket roll. He is looking at a lead slug in his hand.

SHILOH: *(weakly)* Think I'll keep this... We're mighty grateful to you, folks.

WIGGS: You can show it by clearing out before sun-up.

SHILOH: Certain, certain...that is, if I'm fit to travel...otherwise... but let's talk about it in the mornin'...I'm tired.

Wiggs looks at him in helpless anger, but Travis takes his arm and leads him away. Hall starts to follow, picking up the second, half-consumed bottle of elixir. Shiloh, for all his seemingly shut eyes, puts out a hand and clutches the bottle.

SHILOH: You can leave that!

Hall follows Sandy et al away. Shiloh opens one eye and watches them craftily.

SHILOH: *(to boys)* Yessir, real providential...

JESSE: What you mean, Uncle Shiloh?

SHILOH: They got grub, ain't they—an' water...an' a doc to tend my arm, an' a wagon for me to rest up in...

REESE: But thet posse'll catch up with us an' then what?

SHILOH: Ain't likely any posse will look for us in a Mormon wagon train, now, is it?

And the Cleggs exchange crooked grins of satisfaction as Uncle Shiloh curls up to sleep.

FADE OUT

43

FADE IN

MEDIUM CLOSE—MEDICINE WAGON—NEXT MORN-ING

Under the professor's watchful scrutiny, Peachtree is carefully painting the final "n" on a new legend emblazoned on the medicine wagon's side—"Painless Surgeon." It is in considerably larger lettering than "Teeth Pulled" and "Hair Restored." As Peachtree steps away from his handiwork, Hall studies the job and gives it a nod of proud approval.

The camera pulls back as Wiggs, followed by Travis and Sandy, canters down the length of the assembling wagon train and continues purposefully toward the last wagon—Wiggs's own wagon—but now given over to the Cleggs.

ANGLE ON CLEGG WAGON

As Wiggs pulls to a stop. Shiloh is propped on some blankets in the tailgate. The "boys" are standing around him.

WIGGS: You ready, Mister Clegg?

SHILOH: Yes sir...Now don't you fret about me, Brother Wiggs.

WIGGS: I don't intend to!

His eyes take in all of them.

WIGGS: Expect you people to go easy on our food, obey orders, watch your language, and keep your distance...

REESE: *(angrily)* You can't talk to us Cleggses that way!

SHILOH: Shut up, Reese...Elder here's been right kind to us-uns...so you mind your manners!

WIGGS: And when you get your strength back, you'll go your own way...Now is that understood?

SHILOH: *(unctuously)* Lord'll bless you for this, brother...He marks the sparrer's fall.

Wiggs merely grunts, wheels his mount and starts off—accompanied by Travis and Sandy—leaving the younger Cleggs glaring after him.

ANOTHER ANGLE ON WAGON TRAIN

As Wiggs, Sandy, and Travis move off, the latter shoots the elder a frowning side glance.

44

TRAVIS: That wasn't healthy, Elder.

Wiggs stops and looks Travis straight in the eye.

WIGGS: You scared of 'em?

TRAVIS: *(without hesitation)* Yes, sir...I am.

The elder grunts and shifts his gaze to Sandy.

WIGGS: How 'bout you, son?

Sandy gulps and speaks out of a dry mouth.

SANDY: Who? Me?

WIGGS: *(matter-of-factly)* That makes three of us...but I'm not letting the Cleggs know it...and I'm not letting my people know it, either...*(gently)* We're still headed for the San Juan...I want us all to get there...Your haul, wagonmaster!

Wiggs and Sandy continue at a canter to the front of the column.

Travis turns and calls:

TRAVIS: LEAD OUT!

ANGLE ON WAGON TRAIN—RAVINE COUNTRY

Travis, in the foreground, sits his horse and watches the wagons move out. The medicine wagon rolls by with Mr. Peachtree driving and Florey and Denver on the seat beside him. The newly painted "Painless Surgeon" sign is clearly visible. The next and last wagon is that given over to the Cleggs. Floyd drives and Reese and Jesse ride alongside.

Travis turns and canters toward the head of the column.

CLOSER ANGLE ON REAR OF CLEGG WAGON

The professor is re-dressing Shiloh's wound. Shiloh, propped in the tailgate of his wagon, takes a bottle of elixir from his lips and offers it to Hall.

SHILOH: Pitch in, Doc...

Hall hesitates.

SHILOH: You're with friends...We ain't Mormons. Drink up!

The professor surrenders and takes the bottle.

HALL: Well...merely medicinally...

He takes a huge swallow of elixir as we:

WIPE TO:

WIDE ANGLE
The wagon train is winding its way over terrain which should convey the suggestion of pathless country, of a maze of almost identical canyons and gullies in which any man not used to the country could wander for months. It is a plateau region with no sharp accents to negotiate.

MEDIUM CLOSE—FEATURING SANDY
He reins in and peers uncertainly at the land ahead. Travis and Wiggs come up beside him.
SANDY: *(puzzled)* Which one did we come through, Travis? Can you remember?
Travis studies the situation.
TRAVIS: *(pointing)* Right through there...
Wiggs shakes his head, completely bewildered.
WIGGS: Don't know how you can tell. It all looks the same to me.
They start again in a slightly altered direction.

WIDE ANGLE
As the wagon train follows the three riders in the direction Travis has indicated.

DISSOLVE

WIDE ANGLE—RAVINE COUNTRY
It is perhaps a few hours later. The train has been halted by some natural bottleneck or obstacle that can only be passed by one wagon at a time, and with some difficulty. Sandy and Travis are assisting Mrs. Ledyard and the grain wagon as it negotiates the barrier.
(Note: This may be an outcropping of rock or a rock arch or an equally picturesque object.)

NEW ANGLE
Sandy and Travis return to the head of the column where Wiggs is waiting beside the Perkins wagon.
TRAVIS: *(calling)* You're next, Mr. Perkins!

46

At that moment the sound of drunken laughter reaches them from off-screen. Wiggs and the boys look off as the sound is repeated.

WIGGS: *(over shoulder, to Perkins)* Wait a minute, Adam...

REVERSE ANGLE—DOWN LINE OF WAGONS
Other Mormons are moving toward the noise which comes from the rear of the column. Sandy, Travis, and Wiggs, mounted, ride through them. Denver and Florey are also hurrying to the rear of the train.

FULL SHOT—RAVINE COUNTRY—NEAR CLEGG WAGON
The professor is drunk. He has taken a theatrical stance on some rocky eminence and is declaiming—to an audience of mocking Cleggs and shocked Mormons—the opening lines of "Cardinal Wolsey's Soliloquy." His own lack of balance emphasizes the danger of the lines about "falling" and adds to the absurdity of the spectacle. An occasional push or prod by Jesse and Reese threaten to make the professor's fall an actual one.

HALL: Nay, then farewell!
I have touched the highest point
of all my greatness:
And, from the full meridian of
my glory,
I haste now to my setting.
I shall fall
Like a bright exhalation in the evening,
And no man see no more!
Farewell, a long farewell, to all my
greatness!

Denver and Florey are first to break through the little group watching the performance. Florey takes in the situation at once.

FLOREY: *(reproachfully)* Oh, Gus!

She runs to him, but Jesse Clegg blocks her path.

JESSE: *(laughing)* Leave him alone...he's doin' fine...

FLOREY: *(struggling to pass)* Come on, Gus.

Now Denver, mad as a hatter, reaches the professor, takes his arm to steady him and furiously faces the Cleggs.

47

DENVER: You ought to be ashamed!...

HALL: Farewell, a long farewell...

> *Jesse frees Florey, but grabs Denver—laughing at her attempts to lead the professor away.*
>
> *Suddenly the loop of a lariat drops around his shoulders, tightens and hurls him backward—sprawling on the ground.*

ANOTHER ANGLE

> *Travis has ridden in, flanked by Sandy and Wiggs, and has expertly roped Jesse. The other three Cleggs whirl on him angrily.*

TRAVIS: *(to Denver)* Take him back to his wagon, Miss Denver.

> *Jesse struggles to release the rope.*

JESSE: Git this rope off me...git it off or I'll blast ya...hear me!

> *Floyd lets his hands drop to his guns.*

FLOYD: Take that rope off my brother!

WIGGS: *(sharply)* Leave it be...

> *He spins on Floyd and his finger stabs out at him as though it contained a gun.*

WIGGS: And keep your hands off those guns...

> *Only Jesse refuses to subside. He squirms to his feet, facing Travis—hate in his eyes.*

JESSE: I'll blast ya...if it's the last thing I...

WIGGS: *(whirling on him)* No, you won't...because you need him alive same as we do...

> *He crosses to Shiloh.*

WIGGS: Can you and your boys find your way through these canyons, Mister Clegg?

> *Shiloh knows he is beaten. Wiggs exploits the slight advantage he has won.*

WIGGS: *(sternly to Cleggs)* Now get back to your wagon! Turn him loose, Travis.

> *Travis slackens his rope and Jesse flings it off. The Cleggs stand uncertainly a moment, then Shiloh grins in a feeble attempt to regain face.*

SHILOH: No hard feelin's, Elder...The boys was just foolin'...

> *With that the Cleggs turn and shuffle toward their wagon. Travis begins coiling his rope.*

TRAVIS: *(to Wiggs)* That was fast thinkin', Elder...

Wiggs merely grunts and looks disgustedly at the medicine show people—especially at Hall as Florey and Denver support him and start leading him away.

WIGGS: *(reproachfully)* Thought better of you people...guess I was mistaken.

He turns and stomps away. Florey looks after him, on the verge of tears, then turns to the wobbly professor.

FLOREY: *(disappointedly)* Oh, Gus...

MEDIUM SHOT—PERKINS WAGON

Elder Wiggs rides up to the front of the wagon. Perkins—Prudence beside him—is shaking his head dolefully.

PERKINS: A shameful and sinful sight...It's the wrath of the Lord, Elder, for having Gentiles among us!

WIGGS: *(angrily)* The Lord'll have to go some to be madder'n I am...but I ain't blaming it on Gentiles...leastways not all of 'em.

PRUDENCE: Mister Owens didn't do anything, Pa.

PERKINS: *(pettishly)* They're all alike...

Sanctimoniously—with half-shut eyes.

PERKINS: Yes, and I prophesy visitations to come and I prophesy...

WIGGS: Save your wind! Brethren can't hear you anyway...

This thought—more than the injunction—snaps Perkins's half-shut eyes open.

WIGGS: Don't take any prophet to predict we got trouble ahead...but that ain't goin' to stop us if the Lord means for us to get there...And I'll lay you two to one...

PERKINS: *(with a gasp)* Elder! Are you betting on the Lord?

WIGGS: You're danged right I am! So lead out!

And as Wiggs rides again to the head of the train,

DISSOLVE

WIDE ANGLE ON WAGON TRAIN—RAVINE COUNTRY

It is late afternoon of the same day and the sky has cleared. The wagon column threads its way across the broken terrain in a long, strung-out line.

ANGLE ON TRAVIS

As he scouts the terrain far ahead of the column. He rides at an easy lope, looking steadily from left to right as he seeks landmarks.

He guides his horse down into a wash and is slowly picking his way through the rocks and puddles of water when the horse stops, shooting its ears forward. Travis quickly dismounts and leads the animal behind a boulder or rock outcropping, cautiously peering down the ravine.

ANOTHER ANGLE

Travis, in the foreground, sees a file of about twelve Navajos appear at the top of the ravine, ride down into it and up the other side. They do not see Travis but as the last Indian reaches the top of the ravine, his pony scents the Texan's horse and turns toward it with a whinny. Travis makes a Pony Express mount, wheels his horse, and spurs out of the ravine in the direction from which he came. The Indians let out a shout and follow in pursuit.

WIDE ANGLE ON TRAVIS AND INDIANS

Travis rides in a wide circle toward the unseen wagon train. Another small party of Indians emerges from behind a ravine or rock outcropping and joins in a converging pursuit, with Travis in the middle of two hard-riding columns of Navajo warriors.

There is no firing as the chase moves across country. One group of Indians moves ahead of the other and forces Travis to alter his course toward the edge of a steep cliff or side of a mesa.

ANOTHER ANGLE ON TRAVIS

He reins in at the edge of the steep drop and turns to look at his pursuers, who are almost upon him. Without hesitation, he puts his mount over the side and rides down the steep, shelving slope of the mesa at a breakneck speed.

The Indians rein in at the top and then slowly pick their way down the side.

Travis reaches the floor of the valley far ahead of the Indians and gallops across the level terrain toward the wagon column in the distance.

CUT TO:

ANGLE ON WIGGS AND SANDY
They ride at the head of the wagon train and rein in sharply at the sound of pistol shots. Travis races toward them, firing in the air. Travis yells to them as he gallops up:
TRAVIS: Navajos! Circle the wagons!
Sandy wheels his mount and shouts down the column.
SANDY: Navajos! Circle the wagons! Women and children take cover!
Jesse and Reese Clegg canter up, their rifles across their pommels. Wiggs takes command, countermanding Sandy's order.
WIGGS: Hold on! Put those rifles away! Got trouble enough. Travis— you talk Navajo?
TRAVIS: *(puzzled)* I can swap horses with 'em...Sandy talks it real good.
Wiggs dismounts, throws his reins to one of the Cleggs, and looks out over the plain.
WIGGS: Come on, then.
Sandy dismounts and he and Travis join the elder. Together the three men start to walk toward the approaching Indians.

CUT TO:

MOVING ON TRAVIS, SANDY, AND ELDER WIGGS
They walk toward the approaching warriors steadily. The drumming of the Indian horses sounds closer and their yipping grows louder with every step the three men take.
WIGGS: *(gently)* Shuck your pistols, boys. What's the Indian word for "howdy"?
Travis and Sandy unbuckle their gun belts and let them fall to the ground without stopping.
TRAVIS: Yah-tah-hay...
WIGGS: *(softly)* Yah-tah-hay...
They stop and throw up their right hands in the traditional gesture of friendship. The sound of approaching horses grows louder.

ANOTHER ANGLE ON WIGGS, TRAVIS, AND SANDY

The war party gallops toward them, apparently unwilling to recognize the upraised arms of the white men. When they are within a few feet, the Indian leader jerks his mount to a standstill and flings up his arm, signaling his men to hold their fire. The dust kicked up by the ponies drifts toward the white men and the Navajo ponies prance and mill excitedly.

WIGGS: Yah-tah-hay!

The Indian looks at the white men arrogantly.

CHIEF: *(grunting)* Yah-tah-hay!

The three lower their arms. The elder speaks to Sandy, but keeps his eyes on the Indian leader.

WIGGS: Tell them we're friends. Tell them we've come in peace.

Sandy translates the words into Navajo. The chief makes an angry reply.

WIGGS: What did he say?

TRAVIS: Near as I c'n make out, he don't much like white men.

SANDY: *(grinning)* Says we're all thieves.

WIGGS: Smarter'n he looks.

Sandy again speaks to the Indian but Wiggs interrupts hastily.

WIGGS: Don't tell him that. Tell him we're Mormons and that we...

The word "Mormon" has a magic effect on the chief and his face brightens.

CHIEF: Mormons?

He turns to the warriors and shouts.

CHIEF: Mormonee! Mormonee!

The others echo the word and suddenly the tension vanishes. Looks of suspicion and hostility give way to smiles of welcome.

The chief jumps to the ground and formally embraces Wiggs. Turning to Sandy, with a broad smile, he says something that brings a grin to the young man's face.

WIGGS: What'd he say?

SANDY: Says the Mormons are his brothers... Says they're not big thieves like most white men—only little thieves.

WIGGS: Huh! Real complimentary, ain't he?

The chief, who has been staring thoughtfully at Travis, speaks again. Travis's expression grows a trifle sheepish and Wiggs notes it. The Indian finishes his short speech and Travis makes an even briefer reply that seems to satisfy the Navajo.

WIGGS: *(curious)* Well, come on... what was it?

TRAVIS: Claims a fella cheated him in a horse trade couple of months ago. Thought I looked like him.

WIGGS: What'd you tell him?

TRAVIS: I told him that me bein' a Mormon, I wouldn't do a thing like that—seein' as we're brothers an' all.

The chief turns to Wiggs and says something in Navajo. Sandy translates.

SANDY: He's invitin' us to their village tonight.

Both he and Wiggs shoot a look toward the band of the warriors who sit their ponies in silence, their faces once again expressionless.

TRAVIS: *(softly)* I think we better go.

DISSOLVE

INDIAN CAMP—NIGHT
A squaw dance is in progress in honor of the Mormon visitors.

SUGGESTED SERIES OF SHOTS:

1. *Close shot—hands beating rhythmically on drums.*
2. *Wider angle. Squaws and bucks stomp and shuffle around a large central fire to the rhythm of the drums and the chant of the singers.*
3. *Wiggs and the Navajo chief—sit cross-legged on the edge of the dance area watching the show. Behind them—some sitting, some standing—are some of the Mormon men and women. They wear half-frightened smiles, women protectively holding their husbands' arms; others are wholeheartedly enjoying the savage spectacle.*
4. *Closer shot—of a small Mormon boy and his sister peeping wide-eyed from beneath the canvas bows of a wagon at this— their first sight of real Indians.*
5. *Full on the dancers and the Mormon group—as a young Indian girl comes up to one of the Mormon youths and playfully starts to pull him out onto the hard-packed dance area. He hesitates, grinning in embarrassment, but two Mormons give him a shove.*

MORMON: *(laughing)* You're it, Charlie!
SECOND MORMON: No backin' out!
CHARLIE: All right, then...
And he prances out onto the dance line and shuffles awkwardly, trying to get the rhythm.

ANGLE
On a stoic line of bucks—the Navajo equivalent of a stag line—standing with folded arms, staring at Charlie and the Indian girl. Only their eyes are bright with Indian amusement. One starts to smile, but quickly wipes it off.

ANGLE ON DANCERS AND MORMONS
Two other squaws dart in among the Mormons, choosing partners. Now the ice is broken and the men begin to enjoy themselves. But none is having a better time than Mrs. Ledyard—for whom a squaw dance seems to have been originated.

CLOSE ON TWO MORMON WIVES
As though driven by a common impulse, they turn simultaneously to each other—frowning uncertainly. The wives don't mind their husbands enjoying themselves, but they don't want them to enjoy it too much.

FULL ON THE DANCE
Firelight gleams from the silver ornaments of squaws and bucks. Faces are flushed with sweat and excitement. The drums beat louder and the chanting swells.

ANGLE ON MEDICINE WAGON
Still under a cloud as a result of the professor's disgrace, the four medicine-show people stand apart, watching the dance. Two grave-faced Navajos come up and peer at the strange wagon—clearly unlike those of the Mormons. Hall sees their interest. He comes forward affably.
HALL: Good evening, my friends! Anything I can do for you?
One Indian points to the lettering on the wagon.

54

FIRST INDIAN: What he say?

HALL: Well! Speak English, do you?

He takes a stance.

HALL: That, my friends, is the red man's boon to the white man!... Those magic words stand for a formula whispered to me on his deathbed by one of your great medicine men—Chief Sitting Horse!

Neither the name nor the speech makes the slightest impression on his audience. The first Indian merely points again to the lettering.

FIRST INDIAN: *(same tone as before)* What he say?

HALL: *(hoping to make an impression)* It says, my friend, Kickapoo Snake Oil.

SECOND INDIAN: Kickapoo no good!

With a grunt, the two Indians turn their backs and walk away. The professor looks after them with obvious chagrin.

HALL: Professional jealousy!

The four Cleggs stroll by on their way to the dance but Jesse pauses before Denver, eyeing her up and down.

JESSE: How 'bout a dance?

DENVER: It's not my music.

Jesse takes her wrist somewhat roughly.

JESSE: Sounds good to me.

Travis appears behind Jesse.

TRAVIS: *(quietly)* The rule at squaw dances is that the lady asks the gentleman.

JESSE: *(challengingly)* Suppose I was to change the rules?

Shiloh steps up to join the group.

SHILOH: *(chidingly)* Now, Jesse! We don't want to make trouble with the wagonmaster.

Jesse releases Denver's wrist and the Cleggs continue on, with Jesse deliberately jostling Travis as he passes him.

JESSE: *(in a threatening undertone)* Don't crowd your luck, mister!

Travis regains his balance and turns to Denver. The girl is grateful, but once again she has seen him take it from the Cleggs. She masks her concern by assuming a hard attitude.

DENVER: Look—you don't have to protect me. I can take care of myself... I'm used to it.

TRAVIS: *(apologetically)* Yes, ma'am. I know... I'm sorry.

DENVER: And I'm not asking for any sympathy, either!... I've done nothing I need to be ashamed of, no matter what you and your friends may think!... We didn't ask to be picked by these mealy-mouthed Bible-shouters!... And we'll be just as glad to get rid of them as...

TRAVIS: *(interrupting)* No call to get mad at me, ma'am.

DENVER: And don't call me "ma'am"!

TRAVIS: *(awkwardly)* No, ma'am...

> *Bewildered by the tirade, Travis beats a retreat toward the dance. Florey moves closer to Denver and eyes her shrewdly.*

FLOREY: Like him, don't you?

DENVER: I don't want to see him full of bullet holes, if that's what you mean.

> *She wheels on the professor.*

DENVER: When do we clear out of all this?

HALL: *(pompously)* Tomorrow. From then on, these people may shift for themselves!

DENVER: Good.

> *But there is little conviction in her tone as she stares unhappily after Travis.*

FULL SHOT—DANCE—ANGLE INCLUDING PRUDENCE AND SANDY ON SIDELINES

The dancers are responding to the throbbing beat of the drums. One Indian girl snatches up a blanket and holds it like a canopy over the head of her partner. His arm goes around her waist and they leave the line of dancers and run out into the darkness.

Another Indian girl makes the same gesture to her partner. He hesitates, then pulls away and unclasps some silver ornament which he gives to the girl. Then he backs out of the dance. The girl laughs and turns to find a new partner.

MEDIUM CLOSE—PRUDENCE AND SANDY

Prudence watches this byplay. Now she puts her hand on Sandy's arm and gives him a look of frowning inquiry.

PRUDENCE: Why did he give her the silver?

SANDY: *(somewhat embarrassed)* Well, when she put her blanket around him she was sorta suggestin' they get engaged-like.

PRUDENCE: Oh—and when he gave her the silver pin it was like giving her an engagement ring.

SANDY: Oh no! Just the opposite... He didn't care to—so he bought hisself off.

Prudence nods thoughtfully—but has no chance to pursue the inquiries as an Indian girl runs smilingly up to Sandy, catches his hand and tries to pull him out onto the dance area. Sandy hesitates, looks at Prudence, then quickly takes a silver dollar from his pocket and gives it to the Indian girl. The girl takes it and smilingly goes after someone else. Sandy looks at Prudence. She is smiling happily at him. His own smile broadens and with a more assured manner, he takes her arm possessively in his.

FULL SHOT ON THE DANCE

With Wiggs and the chief sitting in the foreground. A beaming Mrs. Ledyard bounds out of the dance area to face Wiggs.

MRS. LEDYARD: *(joyfully)* Elder... I think these squaw dances are a wonderful idea! We oughta have one every Saturday night in our new colony!

Wiggs winces and Mrs. Ledyard grabs another partner and hauls him into the dancing ring.

Suddenly a commotion off-scene attracts the dancers' attention. There is the sound of scuffling and angry voices. The drums falter, then stop as into the firelit area comes a tall young Indian, holding the struggling Reese Clegg with an armlock. An Indian girl—with a torn blouse—follows them. With an easy gesture, the young Indian spills Reese to the ground in front of the chief and Wiggs, and, in angry tones, points from Reese to the girl—clearly accusing him of attack.

The mood of the dance is shattered. There is an angry murmur from the Navajos. The women step back and all the forefront is filled by the men crowding menacingly in upon Reese and regarding the other whites with hostile eyes.

REESE: *(whiningly)* Was only jokin'... didn't mean no harm.

For answer the angry young Indian pulls his wife forward, shows her torn blouse, the finger-bruises on her shoulder. At this further proof, the Indians take a menacing step closer. Reese comes to a half-sitting position, looking from side to side like a cornered rat.

REESE: You keep away from me, you hear... Floyd! Jesse!

But as the Cleggs start to move, Wiggs takes command. He waves them back.

WIGGS: Stand back...

He looks at the Mormon men standing near.

WIGGS: Brother Jamison... Brown... Sam... Take him!

The Mormons purposefully stride forward. For a moment Reese thinks he has been given a personal bodyguard and he gets to his feet. But Wiggs dispels the idea. With a swift motion, he grabs both sides of Reese's shirt and peels it down, stripping him to the waist.

WIGGS: Tie him to a wheel!... Brother Schultz...

As the burly blacksmith Schultz steps forward, Wiggs unbuckles his belt and hands it to him. The other Mormons have grasped Reese's arms and pull him—struggling toward a wagon where they lash his outstretched wrists to a wheel.

Uncle Shiloh steps forward, with Jesse and Floyd at his side.

SHILOH: You ain't whippin' no Cleggses!

The Indians stand watchfully—conscious of this conflict within the white men's group, waiting to see which side will prevail.

Travis moves quickly in front of Shiloh.

TRAVIS: *(quietly)* A whippin's better than a scalpin'.

SHILOH: Ain't goin' to be no scalpin' either!

TRAVIS: *(still quietly)* Think you can stop 'em?

Clegg looks slowly around the semi-circle of Indians.

TRAVIS: It's his hide... or yours!

Clegg hesitates and Wiggs, who has not even looked at him, but has stood waiting for the tying up to be completed, speaks with cold authority.

WIGGS: Lay on, Brother Schultz.

ANGLE ON WAGON WHERE REESE IS TIED TO A WHEEL
Schultz swings back the elder's stout belt and lays on.

ANGLE ON INDIANS AND MORMONS
As the sound of the whipping continues, the Navajos relax and turn

58

to stare with approval at the sight of the white man's punishment. The Indian whose wife was attacked stalks away toward their hogan and the woman follows him.

CLOSE ON SHILOH—WITH JESSE AND FLOYD STANDING BY

Shiloh's mouth jerks with every stroke of the belt, as though he himself were being whipped. Jesse and Floyd exchange glances of concern and, as though moved by a common impulse, take Shiloh's arms and try to lead him away. But Shiloh angrily shrugs their hands off—resolved to see it through.

ANGLE ON WAGON

Schultz hauls back for another stroke, but suddenly Reese's body goes limp and he sags, his weight hanging on his wrists. Schultz leans in and pulls his face around.

SCHULTZ: *(calling to Wiggs)* He is outgone, Elder!

ANGLE ON WIGGS AND NAVAJO CHIEF

WIGGS: *(calling back)* Thank you, Brother Schultz...
He turns and faces the Navajo chief, as if to be sure the Indians are satisfied with the punishment. The Navajo solemnly puts a hand on Wiggs's shoulder and says a few words in Navajo—obviously expressing satisfaction with white man's justice.

WIGGS: *(in reply)* I'm sorry it happened, Brother Lammanite.
Then he turns generally to the Mormons.

WIGGS: Let's get some sleep, folks.

FULL SHOT

The Mormons start away to their wagons and the Indians silently move off in the opposite direction. Wiggs takes a few steps, having to hike his trousers as he goes. The Cleggs cut across toward the wagon where Reese is tied. Wiggs hikes his trousers again, then clutches the waistline and turns.

WIGGS: *(calling)* Give me my belt, Brother Schultz!
Schultz hurries up and hands it to him and Wiggs matter-of-factly starts putting it through his belt loops as he continues away.

ANGLE ON WAGON

Shiloh and Jesse cut Reese down. He is still unconscious. Floyd comes up with a bucket of water and sloshes it over him. Reese groans and stirs. Shiloh looks vengefully after the parting Mormons.

SHILOH: They goin' to wish they never did this!

He turns as Floyd helps the groggy Reese to his feet. Shiloh stares at him a moment and then all his pent-up rage has to find an outlet. He whips an open-handed slap against the side of Reese's jaw, knocking him back against the wagon. Reese's face is a study in bewilderment.

SHILOH: *(whiningly)* Doggone, boy!...I tole you to mind your manners!

FADE OUT

FADE IN

PORTRAIT STUDY—MORNING

Sihouetted against the skyline, their hands raised in a gesture of farewell, are the Navajo chief and a dozen of his braves.

FULL SHOT

From the front of the moving wagon train, toward the distant Indians on the skyline. Wiggs, Travis, and Sandy are turned on their saddles, answering the Indian salute; then they face front and the march resumes.

ANOTHER ANGLE—ON CLEGG WAGON

Reese and Shiloh sit on the tailgate. Reese has been reloading Uncle Shiloh's pistol. Now he spins the cylinder and hands it back to him. Shiloh takes it, but his attention is on the distant Indians.

SKYLINE SHOT

With a final wave, the Indians turn and disappear over the hill.

ANGLE ON CLEGG WAGON

Shiloh grins wolfishly as he sees them go. He looks at Reese. We need no words to convey the fact that the Cleggs are ready to strike.

ANGLE ON MEDICINE WAGON

The professor is driving and Denver sits on the seat beside him. Her expression is thoughtful, somewhat melancholy. Inside the wagon, possibly briefly seen, are Peachtree and Florey, rearranging things in preparation for their California journey. Denver looks up with swift interest as Travis comes cantering down the line toward their wagon—on the professor's side of it. But as he draws close, she glues her eyes on the trail ahead.
Travis reins in beside the professor.

TRAVIS: Cut-off to California's just ahead.

HALL: Splendid.

Travis glances at Denver, but she isn't looking at him.

TRAVIS: You follow the creek bottom ten miles ... then you'll see two peaks in a line ... I made a map to show you ...

He leans over and hands a folded pencil-sketch to Hall. Denver shoots him a quick glance, then as swiftly stares ahead.

TRAVIS: *(lamely)* Glad we met up with you when we did.

He waits a moment, hoping for some answer. When none is forthcoming, he reins in and lets the wagon pull ahead. Only then does Denver turn and crane her head—leaning out in front of the professor—to look back for him.

FULL SHOT—MEDICINE WAGON

As it passes Travis. Peachtree, visible at the tailgate, gapes as Travis spurs ahead again on the other side of the wagon—the side where Denver sits.

ANOTHER ANGLE ON MEDICINE WAGON

As Travis quietly rides up alongside Denver, who still is leaning over, past the professor, for what she thought was her last look at him. She starts at the sound of his voice.

TRAVIS: Sure hope I'll see you again, Miss Denver.

DENVER: *(resuming her poker-face)* Thanks, but don't bank on it ... We

61

move around... *(with a cynical laugh)* With a medicine show you have to—to keep healthy.

TRAVIS: Tradin' horses you move around too.

He studies her hopefully.

TRAVIS: Good thing about it, though...you get to know the country...like a valley I got in mind...

Now he is poker-faced, staring ahead.

TRAVIS: Man could set up a nice little stock ranch in that valley—if he didn't mind the lonesomeness... Now of course if he had someone to help...

Peachtree and Florey—fascinated by this conversation—have come forward curiously, shamelessly eavesdropping. Travis lets the sentence trail off, pauses for Denver's answer. She knows what's on his mind and isn't having any—however tempting. She reaches down on the floor and picks up Prudence's dusty, scuffed walking shoes. She hands them to Travis.

DENVER: *(brutally)* You can give these back... I like mine better! Don't you?

And she hikes up her skirt and sticks out a foot shod with a tawdry slipper—and seemingly doesn't mind showing a considerable stretch of stocking.

Travis has his answer. His mouth tightens.

TRAVIS: No, ma'am!

He spurs off, passing Wiggs who rides into the shot. Wiggs notes the leg show with frowning displeasure.

WIGGS: *(to professor—curtly)* Here's your turn-off...

The professor pulls in the team and looks off in the indicated direction. Florey pokes her head out the wagon.

WIGGS: Now about this team... I'm not asking payment... but we got a colony out in San Bernardino... You might make a contribution when you're passin' through.

FLOREY: *(earnestly)* We'll do it, Elder...

WIGGS: *(warmly)* I know you will, ma'am.

He turns his horse, but Hall isn't one to let an opportunity pass. He removes his hat and strikes an attitude.

HALL: I should like to take this opportunity, sir, to express to you...on behalf of Miss Phyffe, Miss Denver...

WIGGS: *(gruffly)* That's all right...
  He slaps the near horse's rump.
WIGGS: Luck to ye.
  The team starts off at a line tangent to the train and Wiggs, after staring at it a moment, spurs up front past the moving wagons.

ANGLE ON MEDICINE WAGON—MOVING
  It is a few moments later. Florey climbs out from within the wagon to take her place on the box. The three ride in silence—Hall a little miffed because of his unceremonious parting, Denver trying to force Travis out of her mind, Florey sharing Denver's heartache. The professor's emotions—being the shallowest—are the first to find vocal expression.
HALL: *(defiantly)* We're well rid of them!
  No one answers. He takes a noisy inhalation.
HALL: The air smells better already.
  Still no one pays him the least attention.
HALL: Now we can make some progress!
FLOREY: Oh, shut up, Gus!
  She puts a hand tentatively on Denver's shoulders.
FLOREY: He really meant it, didn't he, kid?
  Denver doesn't reply. All this is Greek to Hall.
FLOREY: He was real nice...I don't think you shoulda turned him down!
HALL: *(irritably)* Turned who, turned what?
FLOREY: *(angrily)* Naturally *you* wouldn't recognize a marriage proposal!
HALL: You mean that—that *teamster?*
DENVER: He's *not* a teamster!
HALL: Teamster, wagonmaster, all the same thing...Members of our profession, my dear, are fated for better things...You stick with A. Locksley Hall and some day...some day...
  He pauses impressively, but Florey breaks in.
FLOREY: *(derisively)* Yeah...some day you may have a medicine pitch of your own!
  The professor turns angrily, but a crack of a shot claims all their attention. They turn and stare.

63

FULL SHOT—FROM THEIR ANGLE

From behind a rock—pistol in hand—rides Floyd Clegg. His smile is mocking.

FLOYD: Turn 'em around, Doc!... You ain't goin' no place.

CUT TO:

MEDIUM CLOSE

Sam Jackson lies unconscious on the ground. Over him stands Reese Clegg, pistol in hand, looking down at the man he has just pistol-whipped. As he steps back, he wipes a bloody trickle from his mouth.

The camera pulls back to reveal that the Cleggs are taking over the wagon train. The Mormons stand huddled—men, women, and children. In front of them, guns ready, are Shiloh Clegg and Jesse. Jesse's shotgun is trained on Travis, Sandy, and Wiggs.

Reese looks challengingly at the defensive group.

REESE: Anyone else want to try it?

No one moves.

Reese crosses to Sam Jackson's horse, which stands nearby, and angrily jerks Jackson's carbine from its saddle holster. Holding it by the barrel, he swings it high over his head and brings it crashing down on a rock outcropping—splintering the stock and firing mechanism. He then tosses it contemptuously onto a small pile of similarly broken weapons.

REESE: That's the last of 'em, Uncle Shiloh.

Sam Jackson groans and stirs a little on the ground. Prudence runs out from the Mormon group and goes to his side.

SHILOH: You're a good boy, Reese... We can all rest easy now.

He turns and the Mormons look off at the sound of the returning medicine wagon.

ANOTHER ANGLE

Past the Mormons and the Cleggs to the approaching medicine wagon. Floyd rides beside it. As the wagon pulls up, Shiloh moves toward it.

SHILOH: *(with broad humor)* Welcome back! How was Californey?

64

He chuckles at his own wit and Reese giggles. The professor clambers down from the wagon. Shiloh resumes—enjoying the role of comic and playing to an appreciative audience of Cleggs.

SHILOH: *(with mock solicitude)* Pains me to spoil your trip, Doc, but I just wouldn't rest easy thinkin' of you folks traipsin' around the country...No tellin' what you'd run into—Injuns—varmints—*(with heavy emphasis)*...maybe even a *posse!*...An' that'd be bad, real bad!

Hall doesn't like the situation and speaks with a sincerity born of fear.

HALL: I assure you, Mister Clegg, I had no intention...

Shiloh's answer is to slap him viciously and without warning across the mouth. Hall reels back, hand going to his face.

SHILOH: *(snarling)* Git over there with the rest of 'em!

As Hall does his bidding, Shiloh regains his bland and unctuous manner and crosses toward Wiggs, Sandy, and Travis.

SHILOH: Wouldn't want a friend o' mine to turn Judas...So, like I was sayin', Elder, we'll stay together 'til we reach the San Juan River...one big, happy family—with your old Uncle Shiloh at the head of it.

TRAVIS: If you're headin' for the Arizona border, there's an easier trail than the one we're takin'.

SHILOH: Likely there is...if a man knew the country...But we don't!...No, we'll just string along with you folks so's we can keep an eye on you...Won't be any trouble, will there, Elder?

Wiggs shrugs resignedly. Shiloh smiles his satisfaction and turns toward Jesse and Floyd. Floyd indicates Sandy and Travis with a jerk of his head.

FLOYD: How 'bout their guns?

SHILOH: Get 'em!

ANOTHER ANGLE

Floyd pushes past Jesse and confronts the boys, hands hooked in his belt near his guns. Everything about him suggests a challenge. Wiggs, sensing this, steps unobtrusively to one side—to be clear of any shooting.

FLOYD: Let 'em drop!

They hesitate and Sandy darts a sidelong glance at Travis, ready to take his cue from the Texan.

FLOYD: *(challengingly)* Or maybe you want to draw?...

Floyd almost succeeds in goading Sandy into action and Travis—sensing it—quickly loosens his belt and lets his gun drop. Sandy averts his eyes and slowly follows suit.

Floyd and the other Cleggs laugh contemptuously.

ANGLE ON PRUDENCE

As she supports the still-stunned Sam Jackson in a half-sitting position. She is looking with puzzled, hurt eyes at Sandy.

ANOTHER ANGLE—MEDICINE WAGON

Denver, Florey, and Peachtree are staring at the boys. Denver's emotions are mixed. Florey stares at her to see how she has taken the incident. Denver frowns slightly. Florey reaches a sympathetic hand and pats Denver's wrist.

ANGLE ON WIGGS AND MORMON GROUP

Wiggs seems suddenly old and weary. He turns to his people.

WIGGS: All right, brethren, get back to your wagons...

The Mormons, cowed and disappointed, hesitate, then shuffle away. But Shiloh momentarily halts them.

SHILOH: Hold on!... And if you got any ideas about makin' trouble, forget 'em...

He drapes an arm affectionately around Wiggs's shoulder.

SHILOH: 'Cause it'd sorely grieve me to have to kill my good friend the elder!

He lets it sink in. Wiggs pulls away.

SHILOH: *(harshly)* Get 'em rollin'!

DISSOLVE

FULL SHOT—ON MOVING WAGON TRAIN

Sandy and Travis ride well in front of the column with Floyd Clegg following them watchfully at a discreet distance.

MEDIUM CLOSE—MOVING

On Sandy and Travis. Sandy looks at Travis as though about to speak, but changes his mind and continues on uncomfortably, nursing his troubled thoughts. Travis, aware of this, finally speaks.

TRAVIS: All right—get her said.

Sandy opens his mouth as though to speak his piece and then thinks better of it.

SANDY: *(grumbling)* I got nothin' to say.

Travis looks at him squarely.

TRAVIS: We hired as wagonmasters, not gunfighters.

SANDY: Never claimed to be a gunfighter, but I'd a-taken my chance if you'd backed my play.

TRAVIS: Sure, I know you would ... But I'm not stakin' thirty lives on a fool play like that.

SANDY: Thirty?

TRAVIS: *(impatiently)* What'd happen to these folks if we got ourselves killed?... They'd starve 'fore they found their way over the mountains... or die o' thirst tryin' to make it back to Crystal City... Without us, they haven't got a chance.

SANDY: *(still dissatisfied)* But what happens when we reach the San Juan?... You think the Cleggs are just goin' to tip their hats and ride away?

TRAVIS: Like the elder says—we can worry about that when we come to it.

Sandy looks thoughtful digesting Travis's words.

INTERIOR—MEDICINE WAGON

Florey is putting a wet compress on the professor's split lip while Peachtree, with Denver beside him on the wagon seat, drives. Florey is all mother, fussing over her hurt child.

FLOREY: *(scornfully)* Cleggs!... Brute animals, that's what they are!... *(with sudden concern)* Did he break your uppers?

With swift alarm, Hall puts an exploratory finger to his bridgework.

HALL: No.

FLOREY: Well, that's a blessing.

She starts to shift away, but Hall takes her hand. He is suddenly no

more than what he is—an aging man, a failure, a weakling.
HALL: *(plaintively)* Florey...?
She comes back to him. He looks at her, entreaty in his face.
HALL: Florey, do you wish you were back in stock?... If you do, I still have connections—a few—who still remember me... I could put in a word.
Florey pats his cheek, as a mother would a child's.
FLOREY: *(tenderly)* I don't regret a day we've had together, Gus.
Hall pats her hand awkwardly and turns away to hide his emotion.

EXTERIOR MEDICINE WAGON
Florey pokes her head out of the wagon, close to Denver's. She wears a strangely happy and tranquil smile. She speaks for Denver's ear alone.
FLOREY: You're going to think I'm crazy... but I'm glad they brought us back.
Denver makes no reply. For a moment both women are engrossed in their own thoughts. Then Hall appears beside Florey. She looks at him with some concern. He seems stronger now and more purposeful.
FLOREY: Whyn't you rest, Gus?
HALL: *(soberly)* I've learned a lot in the course of my lifetime, Florey... and one thing I know is that a gun is no better than the man who holds it... The Cleggs don't count for much.
Both Florey and Denver have turned and listened to this with surprise, respect, and hope.

WIDE ANGLE
The wagon train moves on, winding through foothills at the base of a forbidding range of mountains.

WIPE TO:

FULL SHOT
On a distant hill the six-man posse seen earlier leaving Crystal City is drawn up, staring off and down. The marshal, mounted on the skittish Indian pony sold him by Travis, raises a pair of binoculars

and attempts to focus them. The pony skitters, making it impossible for the marshal to keep his glasses trained.

MARSHAL: *(angrily)* Doggone jughead!

FIRST DEPUTY: Whyn't you get off him an' look?

MARSHAL: *(exploding)* 'Cause it's too much trouble gettin' back on ...
He passes the glasses over to a deputy.

MARSHAL: Here, see if you can make 'em out.
The deputy peers through the glasses.

DEPUTY: Looks like that Mormon train left Crystal City.

MARSHAL: Not likely they've seen the Cleggs, but it won't hurt to ask.

ANGLE AT FRONT OF MORMON WAGON TRAIN

Travis and Sandy are being herded back to the wagons by Floyd. They pull up at the first wagon, which is driven by Wiggs with Shiloh sitting beside him. In a moment Reese and Jesse ride in from the flanks. They are all looking curiously at Floyd.

FLOYD: *(calling as he rides in)* Think it's the posse!

CLOSER ANGLE FAVORING WAGON BOX

Uncle Shiloh reacts like an experienced field general.

SHILOH: Jesse, get in here with me ... Reese, you take the Perkins wagon ... Floyd, you ride with the Doc ... And one wrong move from anyone, we start shootin' ... You boys understand that?
Travis and Sandy nod.

SHILOH: Then ride out front where we can see you! ...
Floyd and Reese spur off, taking Jesse's horse. Jesse swings into the wagon and follows Shiloh back into the body.

ANGLE FROM INTERIOR WAGON—SHOOTING OUTWARD

Shiloh is crouched on the floor of the wagon and has his gun trained on the elder's back. Sandy and Travis are framed in the wagon bows, moving in front of his wagon. The marshal and the posse ride up, the marshal surprised to see the boys traveling with the Mormons.

MARSHAL: *(sourly, to boys)* Oh, it's you two! What happened—you get religion?

The boys make no answer and the marshal continues to Wiggs.
MARSHAL: Howdy!...Didn't think you'd make it this far.
WIGGS: We been movin' along.
MARSHAL: We're still huntin' those Cleggs...Don't suppose you've seen 'em?
Wiggs hesitates, but Shiloh rams a gun barrel in the small of his back.

ANOTHER ANGLE—FAVORING WIGGS AND MARSHAL
WIGGS: *(noncommittally)* Doesn't seem likely now, does it?
MARSHAL: Nope—had to ask, though...Happen you see 'em, I'd appreciate your gettin' word to me. We're campin near the old California cut-off... *(complacently)* Them Cleggses ain't goin' to slip past us.
One of the deputies works his horse over close to the marshal's.
DEPUTY: *(to marshal)* How about the bacon?
MARSHAL: *(suddenly remembering)* Oh, yeah... *(to Wiggs)* We're runnin' low on grub...don't s'pose you'd have an extra side of bacon in there?
He jerks his thumb to the wagon.
WIGGS: *(hesitantly)* Why...yes...guess so.
MARSHAL: Mighty grateful!
The deputy starts to dismount, as though to board the wagon. Wiggs shoots Travis a look of warning. Travis at once spurs close and dismounts.
TRAVIS: *(quickly)* I'll get it.
As Travis climbs into the wagon:
MARSHAL: *(to Wiggs—his manner somewhat friendlier):* Still say it, mister...You'll never get your wagons through those mountains... Some traders tried it two years ago...

INTERIOR WIGGS'S WAGON
Travis is crawling past the watchful figure of Jesse in his search for the bacon as the marshal's voice drones on faintly. The marshal's words probably need not be heard but this is what he is saying:
MARSHAL'S VOICE: We couldn't even reach the place where they'd gone

70

over...Then there was another time. Some government surveyors started through...They quit after two months...near dead.

    Travis gets his hands on a canvas-sewn side of bacon and is snaking it down, when Shiloh leans over to whisper.

SHILOH: *(in menacing undertone)* Git rid of 'em—hear!

    Travis continues to the back of the wagon.

EXTERIOR—FRONT OF WIGGS'S WAGON

    As Travis reappears and passes the bacon up to the deputy.

MARSHAL: *(concluding)* So if you take my advice...

TRAVIS: *(meaningful emphasis)* Think we'd better get rollin', Elder.

WIGGS: *(to Travis)* Yeah...

    He turns to the marshal.

WIGGS: *(humbly)* We'll be all right, marshal, 'cause we ain't travelin' alone...

    Sandy and Travis stiffen and Wiggs's body jerks—and we must know that Shiloh has shoved the gun barrel against his spine. But Wiggs—after a brief pause—resumes levelly.

WIGGS: The Lord's ridin' along with us.

    He slaps the reins across the team and the wagon moves on. The camera holds on the marshal and his posse. The marshal pushes his hat back from his forehead and scratches his head bewilderedly, staring after the wagon.

MARSHAL: *(reflectively)* I swear, I'll never understand them!

    As the next wagon passes, the marshal turns and looks down the line. He stares at what he sees.

ANOTHER ANGLE

Shooting from behind the medicine wagon and toward the marshal and posse. The marshal rides in.

MARSHAL: *(calling—surprised):* What are you people doing here?

CLOSER ANGLE—MEDICINE WAGON BOX AND MARSHAL

With the posse trailing. Hall is driving, with Peachtree and Denver alongside.

MARSHAL: Thought I'd seen the last of you!

Peachtree politely spits.
MARSHAL: Thought you were going to California! Don't you know the cut-off's back there?

INTERIOR WAGON
Floyd, shielded by Florey, has a gun at Hall's back. He prods Hall into speech.
HALL: *(glumly)* We changed our mind.

FIRST ANGLE—MEDICINE WAGON BOX AND MAR-SHAL
MARSHAL: *(with a look at Denver)* Figurin' on turning Mormon, maybe?
Florey leans out from inside the wagon. She winks impudently at the marshal.
FLOREY: *(archly)* Can't blame him, can you, Marshal?
The posse whoops its appreciation.
MARSHAL: *(laughing)* No, ma'am!
And, chuckling over the situation, the marshal and the posse ride up again toward the front of the column. But Florey's smiling mask drops as Floyd's rough hand grabs her shoulder and pulls her down again within the wagon.

ANOTHER ANGLE—MOVING WAGON TRAIN
As the posse spurs up front. The marshal slows as he notes a saddled buckskin horse tied to the tail of the Perkins wagon. It is Reese's mount. The marshal studies it with interest, then resumes his course toward the front.

ANOTHER ANGLE—HEAD OF TRAIN
Sandy and Travis, and Wiggs on his wagon. As the marshal rides in:
MARSHAL: *(calling)* Whose buckskin horse is that tied to the next wagon...?
As Travis looks back...
MARSHAL: *(sharply)* Seen it somewheres afore...
TRAVIS: *(easily)* Sure did! Tried to sell him to you once!... You can still have him cheap!

72

The marshal is suddenly reminded of Travis's other horse deal.
MARSHAL: *(angrily)* Mister, you've taken your last dime off me!
He returns angrily to Wiggs's side.
MARSHAL: If I was you, Elder, I'd be more careful who I took up with! There's some mighty unsavory characters travelin' with this wagontrain!
WIGGS: *(with a faint smile)* That's the Lord's truth, Marshal.
MARSHAL: *(to posse)* Well, let's go back to where we can keep an eye out for those Cleggs!
The posse rides away.
Shiloh cautiously pokes his head above the wagon seat behind Wiggs and then, cackling with laughter, slides up alongside.
SHILOH: Slick, mighty slick!... I can see we ain't going to have no trouble!

DISSOLVE

WIDE ANGLE SHOT—A FEW MINUTES LATER
Showing the posse as it climbs a ridge in the broad afternoon sunlight, veering off from the moving wagon train just as it enters the long shadow cast by the mountain. The posse pulls up and looks back at the wagon train until the last wagon in the caravan disappears into the shadow—which is, in a sense, symbolical of the loneliness and isolation to which the wagon train is committed.

FULL SHOT—WAGON TRAIN
As it winds its way up a narrow ravine whose sheer walls tower high above. Again the effect to be sought is one of man's puniness in the face of a monstrous and threatening Nature.

MEDIUM CLOSE—WAGON BOX—WIGGS AND SHILOH
Shiloh scans the towering walls and overhanging rocks with fear-filled eyes and almost superstitious awe. Wiggs, on the other hand, guides his wagon with serene confidence in the Lord. Shiloh suddenly looks ahead fearfully as the sound of sliding, falling stones comes over scene.

ANGLE—SHOOTING PAST SHILOH TOWARD TRAVIS AND SANDY

The boys have pulled up their horses, while Travis has thrown a hand high signaling a halt. A shower of rubble, including three or four rocks the size of a man's head, slides into the ravine a few yards ahead of them. The boys wait for the dust to lift and to see whether another slide is coming. When nothing happens, Travis brings down his hand in the forward signal and they move into the drifting dust kicked up by the slide.

DISSOLVE

FULL SHOT—COLUMN—DUSK

As the column emerges from the head of the ravine and pulls up onto a small plateau at the base of the mountain.

Sandy and Travis sit their horses and wait for Wiggs's wagon to come up.

TRAVIS: This is about as good a stopping place as we're going to find before dark.

WIGGS: *(tiredly)* All right, son...

He clambers stiffly down from the wagon, followed by Shiloh. Sandy and Travis dismount. The other Mormon wagons come up in the background. All four men stand and slowly raise their eyes— up and up and up—toward the reaching mountains they must surmount.

SHILOH: *(incredulously)* You mean to say we got to cross *them?*

Travis nods.

SHILOH: *(his fear manifest)* Ain't there some kinda pass?

Travis shakes his head and grins faintly, seeing Shiloh's alarm.

TRAVIS: Might be safer facin' that posse, Mister Clegg.

SHILOH: *(eyes narrow)* You keep talkin' that way, son, an' you won't be any safer than the elder here!

Shiloh gives Wiggs a shove toward the assembling Mormons in the background. Wiggs stumbles as Shiloh follows him. Travis and Sandy look after them, then turn to face each other. If they had any doubt about Shiloh's intention to kill the elder, it has been settled now.

74

DISSOLVE

FULL SHOT—MORMON ENCAMPMENT—NIGHT

The Mormons sit about their campfires under the watchful eyes of the Cleggs. Their attitude is in marked contrast to their former demeanor. There is no singing, no conversation. A fretful child is quickly quieted by its mother. One of the Mormon men stands— Floyd Clegg gets quickly to his feet, watchful. The man merely goes to his wagon, takes a canteen and drinks. Floyd watches warily. The man returns to his former place and only then does Floyd relax and sit down. A few Mormons mend harness or do other minor tasks, but they work listlessly, dejectedly.

ANOTHER ANGLE

Sandy, Travis and the professor are playing a desultory game of poker—playing obviously to kill time, not with any interest in it. Not far away sits Reese Clegg.

SANDY: *(in whisper)* Maybe I could sneak off, get the posse.

TRAVIS: *(whisper)* Not much chance...anyway, you'd be missed... They'd kill the elder right off!

SANDY: *(loudly, forgetfully)* Well, ain't they anyway!?

Reese looks sharply at them, stands as though to start over, then hesitates.

HALL: *(loudly)* I'll bet three.

TRAVIS: *(normal)* Stayin'...*(quietly)* That depends on us.

Reese re-settles himself and barely turns his head as young Billy Jamison climbs down out of his parents' wagon and, followed by his dog, walks with an air of almost too-elaborate casualness toward the card players.

Travis absently reaches a hand to pat the dog.

CLOSER ANGLE

The boy kneels beside Travis and, with a swift look, to make sure he is not observed, opens his coat to show Travis the old pistol stuck into the waistband of his trousers.

BILLY: *(in whisper)* They didn't find it!

    Travis moves as though to take it, but the boy's next words stop him.

BILLY: It isn't loaded... Pa wouldn't buy me any bullets.

ANOTHER ANGLE

On the card players, with Reese in the background. The men exchange glances of stunned disappointment. At that moment, Reese starts toward them. Travis quickly closes Billy's coat over the gun.

TRAVIS: All right, Billy... You get on back to your wagon.

    Billy quickly gets to his feet and with a guilty air starts away. Reese looks after him, frowning.

REESE: *(calling)* Whoa there, you!

    The youngster freezes—clearly tempted to run, but he realizes it would be in vain. Slowly he turns as Reese stalks over to him. The group at the card game stares in dismay.

REESE: Watcha call yer dawg?

BILLY: *(stammering)* T... T... Teddy.

    Reese reaches down and pats the dog's head roughly.

REESE: Nice dawg.

    Boy and men relax.

ANOTHER ANGLE

Favoring Hall as he plucks three walnut shells from a pocket and starts intoning the usual spiel as he starts practicing a shell game.

HALL: Hand is quicker than the eye... Now you see it, now you don't... Find the pea... That's all there is to it.

    Reese turns curiously and the professor repeats the performance—somewhat to the mystification of Sandy and Travis.

HALL: A game of skill... so simple a child can play... Where is the pea?

    Reese has hunkered down beside the professor and stares fascinated. When the shells come to rest, he places a finger on one of them.

REESE: Here!

HALL: I am sorry, sir...

    He turns the indicated shell over.

HALL: Yes, I know...a bean is a small thing...something larger perhaps, say, one of these.

> *And Hall neatly plucks a cartridge from Reese's gun belt and places it on the playing surface. He covers it with a walnut and begins to shuffle it. Sandy and Travis suddenly have realized what the professor's game is—and exchange quick glances.*

HALL: Now you see it...Now you don't...

> *Reese's finger pounced on one of the shells.*

REESE: There she is!

HALL: Too bad, my friend! Shall we try again?

WIDER ANGLE
> *Reese stands in disgust.*

REESE: *(growling)* Nah!

> *He starts away, but then remembers.*

REESE: *(returning with hand outstretched)* Gimme back my bullet!

> *Hall grasps Reese's hand and uses it to pull himself erect and then— very politely—he replaces the bullet in Reese's gun belt.*

HALL: *(during this)* Of course! How forgetful of me!

> *Reese merely grunts an acknowledgment and walks away. Sandy and Travis get dejectedly to their feet.*

SANDY: Well, it almost worked.

HALL: *(calmly)* Quite right!

CLOSER ANGLE
> *And he shows them his other hand. It contains two bullets filched from the back of Reese's belt.*

SANDY: Two!

HALL: Tomorrow's another day...

> *And he turns to head for the medicine wagon—and a night's sleep.*

FADE OUT

FADE IN

WIDE ANGLE—DAY

The wagon train is zig-zagging up the side of a mountain—the wagons canted at a dangerous angle as they negotiate the steep ascent. In most cases, women are driving while men and boys walk alongside the teams, pulling on bridles.

Perhaps one or two men on horseback have their ropes made fast to a wagon, bracing their weight against it to keep the wagon from tumbling downhill.

ANOTHER ANGLE

Accentuating the dizzy height which the wagon train has attained. Wagon after wagon reaches a small shelf or plateau. Horses and men tremble with exhaustion as they come to a halt.

FULL SHOT

The grain wagon, last in the column, is still toiling up the slope. Sam Jackson, his head bandaged, is on the driver's box. Sandy and three of the young Mormon wranglers have made their lariats fast to the sides of the wagon and to the pommels of their saddles. Their horses strain upward, assisting the almost spent team. The men are shouting encouragingly to one another and Jackson is urging his team onward. With a final lunge, the wagon crests the plateau and pulls up beside Elder Wiggs's wagon. Wiggs is on the seat with Shiloh. They are both looking up and off.

FULL SHOT—FROM WIGGS'S ANGLE

Down a precipitous slope rides Travis, who has been ahead scouting out the terrain. He works his horse down through sliding rubble and lopes across the intervening space to the Wiggs wagon. As he passes the grain wagon, Jackson calls.

JACKSON: We goin' to stop a while?

TRAVIS: *(calling)* No time.

ANOTHER ANGLE

As he joins Wiggs and Shiloh.

TRAVIS: Goin' to have to double-span, Elder.

WIGGS: All right, son.

Travis dismounts and looks around for Sandy.

TRAVIS: *(calling)* Sandy...lend a hand!

And as he walks off, Wiggs climbs down, moves toward the front of his team, preparing to double-span. Floyd walks his horse over. His manner is apprehensive.

FLOYD: Wouldn't ride wagon if I was you, Uncle Shiloh... Horse be a lot safer.

SHILOH: *(starting to climb down)* Thank ye, Floyd.

WIGGS: Fightin' man like you wouldn't be scared, would he?

Shiloh Clegg glares at him, but settles back into the wagon seat.

SHILOH: *(softly—but with menace):* Talk while you kin, Elder!

ANGLE ON MEDICINE WAGON

Travis and Sandy assist Peachtree in bringing another team in line and double-harnessing it to the medicine wagon. Hall sidles up to Travis and carefully shields his palm.

CLOSE ON HALL

Revealing that he now has three bullets in the palm of his hand.

HALL: Mr. Floyd Clegg made a small contribution.

ANOTHER ANGLE

Travis looks up swiftly as Jesse rides up behind the professor.

TRAVIS: *(hurried undertone)* Careful!

JESSE: Hurry it up!

The professor eyes Jesse's gun belt and moves toward him. He extends a hand toward Jesse's saddle.

HALL: *(casually)* I say, that's an interesting saddle.

Jesse slaps his hand with his reins.

JESSE: *(curtly)* Keep your hands to yourself!

And he rides away. Hall looks after him disappointedly, and shrugs resignedly as Travis and Sandy—who have taken in this byplay— cross back to the grain wagon where Sam Jackson stands beside his team.

ANOTHER ANGLE

Grain wagon and medicine wagon in background.

TRAVIS: Hitch your team to the Jamison wagon.

SAM JACKSON: *(protesting)* And leave the grain here?

SANDY: *(conciliatory)* We're comin' back for it.

SAM: *(unconvinced)* The grain ought to go first!

    He glares off at the medicine wagon, gestures in its direction.

SAM: *(loudly)* It's more important than they are!

    The medicine show people turn hearing this—and stand waiting. Travis and Sandy, who know what chances the professor has been taking, would like to defend him, but cannot.

TRAVIS: *(quietly)* We're still the wagonmasters!

    Sam looks them up and down with something like contempt, but he turns and starts unhitching the team.

REVERSE ANGLE

Past the medicine wagon, toward the grain wagon. Denver stands in the foreground as Travis leaves Jackson unhitching his team and comes up to her.

TRAVIS: Don't mind Mister Jackson... We'll get you through.

DENVER: *(smiling a little)* I'm not worried.

TRAVIS: That's right... Reckon I'm worryin' enough for two.

    And as he joins Peachtree near the teams...

WIDE ANGLE—PLATEAU

Four of the wagons stand double-spanned—Wiggs's, Jamison's, Perkins's, and the medicine wagon—while the others stand with dropped wagon tongues. The women and children belonging to the wagons about to make the ascent leave the main group and toil up ahead; the others group about their wagons, watching.

DRIVERS: *(ad lib—calling)* Ready... All ready...

TRAVIS: *(calling)* Lead out, Elder Wiggs...

    Now begins the most grueling part of the ascent. Each wagon is pulled by from six to eight horses. Outriders—with their ropes made fast to the tops of the wagons—ride above them, on the up-slope, trying to preserve the wagons' balance.

    Men and horses strain to make the almost impossible climb, drivers exerting every ounce of strength and skill to get the most out of their teams.

SERIES OF SUGGESTED SHOTS:

1. *Close on a wagon wheel—as it bites into the loose shale and barely turns.*
2. *Three or four men, throwing their weight against the back of one wagon, pushing it forward.*
3. *Angle—on middle-aged Mormon driver—six lines grasped in his hands—as he skillfully guides his team, calling his horses by name.*
4. *Angle—from above the wagon, accentuating the grade, showing the figures of the watching Mormons below as they peer up.*
5. *Angle on Wiggs's wagon—Wiggs is working his horses with an expression of confidence, almost eagerness. Shiloh, on the other hand, is hanging desperately to a support, his terror manifest.*
6. *Sandy, afoot, walks on the uphill side of Wiggs's off-lead horse, leading the column and guiding Wiggs's team. Far up ahead of him may be seen a level stretch of shelf that is their immediate objective.*
7. *Shot from far below—where the abandoned wagons stand— toward the tiny wagons inching their way up the mountain. Trailing the wagons, on foot, are the women and children.*
8. *The women and children toil uphill, while Jesse Clegg—his shotgun across the pommel of his saddle—follows them watchfully on horseback. A woman stumbles and falls. Jesse reins in but merely waits—not offering her any assistance—until she gets to her feet again and resumes her climb.*
9. *On the stretch of level ground, Floyd Clegg stands— dismounted—watching the approach of Wiggs's wagon. His expression is impatient.*
10. *Sandy and the lead team reach the shelf and pass Floyd Clegg, who reluctantly moves aside to make way for them. As the wagon comes to a halt, Floyd helps the shaky Shiloh down to the ground. Shiloh's legs almost buckle.*

FLOYD: *(ribbing Shiloh)* What kept you?

Shiloh cackles nervously, one fist wiping his mouth.

SHILOH: Heh!... Heard what that marshal said?... Said she couldn't be clumb... But Shiloh Clegg clumb her!

He tries to spit triumphantly, but not a drop of spittle comes out.

SHILOH: Dry!... *(he extends his hand)* Need a chaw, boy.

Floyd hands him a plug and Shiloh shakily bites off a chunk.

WIDER ANGLE
As the other wagons come to a rest on the plateau, Sandy starts to unbuckle the harness on the Wiggs wagon. Sam Jackson passes and Sandy calls to him.

SANDY: Lend a hand, will you!

As Jackson comes over, followed by Travis, Shiloh turns toward them frowning.

SHILOH: What you doing?

SANDY: Goin' to bring up the rest of the wagons.

SHILOH: No, you ain't either! Wasted enough time... You can tell those folks to start walkin'!

WIGGS: Mister Clegg, we need those wagons.

Shiloh spits. Jackson angrily bends again to his task. Shiloh glares at him.

SHILOH: *(to Jackson)* You heard me! Said leave 'em be.

Jackson straightens defiantly.

JACKSON: I'm going after that grain wagon... *(calls ahead)* Lead 'em out!

WIDER ANGLE
Sandy leads the horses out and turns them around, facing the downslope. As he comes abreast of Jackson, Jackson takes the lead reins.

Shiloh signals Floyd to stop them.

SHILOH: *(with an indicative gesture)* Floyd!

Floyd draws his gun and steps forward, toward Sandy and Jackson. As they hesitate, Travis steps up and takes his place beside them—facing Floyd and Shiloh.

TRAVIS: *(levelly)* Our deal was to get these wagons through... We aim to live up to it... and if you Cleggs figure you don't need guides, start shootin'... *(he pauses)* Come on, Mister Jackson...

Without a backward look, Travis takes the guide lines and, accompanied by Jackson and Sandy, starts down the slope. Other Mormons in the background follow their lead.

82

Floyd looks at Shiloh for instruction. Shiloh makes a gesture as though telling him to put his gun away. Floyd slowly obeys. Wiggs grins.

WIGGS: *(to Shiloh)* Seems you got a bull by the tail. You can't let go!

MEDIUM CLOSE—JACKSON, TRAVIS, AND SANDY
As they lead the horses down the slope.

JACKSON: *(earnestly)* I'm apologizing... I'm apologizing to you both. *The boys nod their acknowledgement.*

WIPE TO:

FULL SHOT—PLATEAU
As the grain wagon, drawn by six or eight horses, pulls up the slope, passing Wiggs, Shiloh, and Reese. Sam Jackson is on the driver's seat and Sandy and Travis are helping the horses hold their footing.

CLOSER ANGLE—ON SHILOH AND WIGGS
As the grain wagon passes with the bulging grain sacks visible through the tailgate.

SHILOH: *(sneeringly)* You'd think there was pure gold in them sacks.

WIGGS: Means more than gold to us...
He pauses and looks at Shiloh.

WIGGS: ...but your kind wouldn't understand that.
Shiloh looks sharply at Wiggs and then back at the grain wagon with new interest in his eye. He has found the weapon that will defeat Wiggs and the Mormons—the grain.

SHILOH: *(thoughtfully)* Mebbe not...

DISSOLVE

WIDE ANGLE ON MOUNTAIN CAMP—NIGHT
A cold wind beats at the figures huddled around sheltered campfires. The day's climb has turned them into a bone-weary group. Not even the Cleggs are immune. Uncle Shiloh, enshrouded in a blanket, sits slumped, his head nodding. Reese is fully asleep. Only Jesse and Floyd maintain a vigil, but Floyd has to pull himself

awake by sheer force of will. Wiggs, Sandy, and Travis sit at a nearby fire.

Jesse gets stiffly to his feet and starts for the medicine wagon. Denver, Peachtree, Florey, and the professor lean against it, bundled against the cold and somewhat apart from the Mormons.

FULL SHOT—ON MEDICINE WAGON GROUP

As Jesse walks up to them. Florey looks at him with open dislike.

FLOREY: What do you want?

JESSE: Some of that pain-killer.

Denver rises suddenly. Her manner is surprisingly cordial.

DENVER: I'll get it.

She gives Jesse a sidelong glance as she steps onto the wagon. Jesse enjoys a passing leg show.

MEDIUM CLOSE ON SANDY, TRAVIS, AND WIGGS

As they stare frowningly off at the medicine wagon. Travis doesn't look too happy. Sandy looks at his friend sympathetically, but says nothing.

ANGLE ON MEDICINE WAGON

As Denver descends with a bottle of Lightning Elixir. Jesse reaches to take it but Denver, her eyes holding Jesse's, takes the first drink before passing him the bottle. As he tilts it to his lips, Denver darts a look at the professor. Florey frowns at her but Hall is clever enough to understand her game.

She takes the bottle from Jesse's hand and holds it up to the firelight. It is only about half full. With a provocative look she reaches back into the wagon and takes out another bottle of elixir, which she offers to Jesse.

JESSE: *(suspiciously)* What's the idea?

DENVER: It's a cold night.

JESSE: Maybe it don't have to be.

He puts a tentative arm around her. She yields slightly. He kisses her, then releases her—with a triumphant laugh he turns toward Travis. Denver puts her arm through Jesse's as though to

84

accompany him back to the Clegg fire. Jesse pulls away and merely takes the bottles.

JESSE: *(with contempt)* I had you pegged from the beginning.
He turns on his heel and starts away.

ANGLE ON TRAVIS—WITH WIGGS AND SANDY
Travis watches Jesse as he rejoins Floyd at the fire. Sandy and Wiggs eye him apprehensively.

MEDIUM CLOSE ON MEDICINE WAGON
Denver stands looking after Jesse. Florey is studying her bewilderedly—unable to understand her behavior. Denver hunches her shoulders, pulls her clothing tighter as though at a sudden chill in the air. Her expression is enigmatic. Slowly she starts for the Travis group.

ANGLE ON TRAVIS WITH WIGGS AND SANDY
Travis sees Denver approach, but after one quick glance deliberately stares into the fire, ignoring her. Wiggs and Sandy give her a hostile look. She comes to a stop in front of Travis, waiting for him to look up at her. When he refuses, she smiles a little bitterly.

DENVER: *(quietly)* I thought you might need these.
One by one, she tosses two bullets onto the ground before him and then, without waiting for an answer, hurries away.

CLOSE ON TRAVIS
As his hand quickly covers the two bullets and as he looks up after her with full realization of what she has done.

DISSOLVE

FULL SHOT—NEXT DAY
On the last two wagons of the train, with Jesse Clegg—mounted and shotgun over his pommel—riding behind them. The wagons have been moving up a fairly steep grade in single file. The next-to-last wagon comes to a sudden halt and the driver of the last wagon has to haul back on his reins to stop his team. Off-screen is a chorus

of excited calls—ad libs, "Whoa" and "What's wrong?," etc.
As the drivers lean out, looking ahead, Jesse Clegg rides past them
curiously.

ANOTHER ANGLE—SHOOTING TOWARD HEAD OF WAGON TRAIN

Mormon men are jumping from their wagons and moving forward
to see what obstacle has stopped the movement of the column. Jesse
Clegg rides through them.

JESSE: *(calling)* Out of the way...stand aside!

ANOTHER ANGLE—AT HEAD OF WAGON TRAIN

As the Mormons make way for Jesse, the open ground ahead is
revealed. The trail has suddenly come to an end. Ahead lies merely
a narrow ledge on the side of the mountain, a ledge barely wide
enough to accommodate a single horseman. On one side of the
ledge, the mountain rises almost sheer; on the other is a drop into a
yawning chasm.
Sandy, Travis, Wiggs, Shiloh, and the other Cleggs—the latter
mounted—stare off at the seemingly impassable barrier. The
Mormon men come up behind them—their faces showing their
dismay and despair at sight of what lies ahead.

ANGLE—FAVORING SANDY, TRAVIS, WIGGS, AND SHILOH

SANDY: Must have been a landslide. That ledge was plenty wide before.

WIGGS: You certain it's the same trail?

TRAVIS: Yessir...it's gotta be. There isn't another one.

Shiloh looks at Wiggs with some satisfaction.

SHILOH: Well, Elder, looks like your wagons have got as far as they're goin' to get.

Sandy tries to offer Wiggs some consolation.

SANDY: Horses could pack some of the load.

Wiggs shakes his head.

WIGGS: But they can't pack ploughs—and without 'em...

He shakes his head, then his voice takes on a note of determination.

WIGGS: No sir! Got to get the wagons over...somehow!

86

SHILOH: *(with brutal finality)* Can't be did! Your luck's run out, Elder.
He winks slyly at Floyd.

SHILOH: Or maybe the Lord never meant you to settle in that valley.
*Wiggs barely shoots him a look and then advances to the very edge
of the chasm.*

PORTRAIT STUDY—WIGGS
WIGGS: Lord, this is me again...Jonathan Wiggs of Utah...
He pauses, thinking of his next words.

WIDE ANGLE—MORMON GROUP
*The Mormons, who have heard this salutation before, know what it
signals. Almost as one, the men remove their hats and men, women,
and children drop to their knees. Sandy and Travis exchange
somewhat sheepish glances and then, as Wiggs's prayer continues,
remove their hats.*
WIGGS: *(off-screen)* Lord, I've heard it said that faith can move
mountains... Bein' a weak an' sinful man, I reckon I just don't have that
kind of faith. But the brethren here...

STUDY OF MORMON FACES
WIGGS: *(off-screen)* ...had faith enough to *cross* mountains when folks
said they couldn't!...

PORTRAIT—WIGGS
WIGGS: Now I'm not one to question Your reasons, Lord, but I can't
believe You'd let us come this far if You didn't mean for us to go all the
way...
He turns back to the Mormons.
WIGGS: Brethren, pray along with me.

ANGLE ON MEDICINE GROUP
*Standing apart from the main Mormon party, the self-conscious
medicine show people are impressed by Wiggs's simple prayer.
Florey drops to her knees and Peachtree, very sheepishly, follows
suit. Hall hesitates, then gets to one knee. Only Denver remains
standing, but her eyes are suspiciously bright and her gaze—like the
elder's—is heavenward.*

87

ANOTHER ANGLE—WIGGS

With Travis, Sandy, and Shiloh in the background. Travis is staring reflectively at the ledge.

WIGGS: *(replacing his hat)* Amen!

Only the Cleggs remain unimpressed. Shiloh deliberately turns and stares at the ledge. He spits a jet of tobacco juice and turns back to Wiggs.

SHILOH: *(with a cackle)* Heh!... It ain't a foot wider'n it was before... Too bad your wagons don't run on a single track!

He smacks Reese on the back, enjoying his own wit. But Travis suddenly spins excitedly from contemplation of the ledge, stares at Shiloh with a glinting eye.

TRAVIS: That's a good idea, Mister Clegg!

They all gape at him. Travis turns to Wiggs.

TRAVIS: You carryin' picks and shovels?

Wiggs nods.

TRAVIS: Get 'em!

He turns to Shiloh, with a slow grin.

TRAVIS: If this dugway works, Mister Clegg, you can consider yourself an angel of the Lord!

Shiloh looks around uncomfortably as his nephews regard him with a touch of superstitious awe and Reese shifts a few inches from him.

QUICK WIPE

FULL SHOT—LEDGE

Travis, backed by Jackson, Schultz, and other Mormons carrying picks and shovels, stands on the ledge. He indicates an imaginary line with his hand across the middle of the ledge.

TRAVIS: Start here... I want a trench just wide enough for a wheel— and at an angle—understand?

The men nod and the picks start swinging.

Travis passes the Cleggs, who look on—curiously, still unconvinced.

FULL SHOT—HEAD OF COLUMN

As Travis rejoins Wiggs.

TRAVIS: We'll have to lighten the wagons... Maybe you can send back for whatever you leave.

Wiggs smiles faintly.

WIGGS: What makes you think I'll be around to send for anything?

Then, covering up quickly.

WIGGS: I'll see what can be spared.

As he moves off, Travis stares after him—knowing that Wiggs is fully aware of his impending death at the hands of the Cleggs. As he stands, the professor joins him and covertly hands him the bullets he has filched from the Cleggs. Travis counts them into his palm, his expression thoughtful.

TRAVIS: That makes five... Five bullets... four Cleggs.

HALL: *(gently)* I used to think five to four was good odds.

He looks off toward Denver, off-screen.

HALL: I hope it doesn't come to a showdown.

Travis turns and looks in the same direction as the professor.

ANGLE ON PERKINS WAGON—FROM TRAVIS'S VIEWPOINT

Including the professor and Travis in the foreground and showing Denver, sitting near Prudence and putting on the dusty pair of stout shoes she had surrendered to Travis once before. Prudence, in her turn, is admiring the fragile slipper Denver has just removed. Denver suddenly catches Travis's eye on her, blushes and ducks her head to fasten her shoe.

TRAVIS: *(thoughtfully answering the professor)* Doc—I hope so, too.

MOVING ON WIGGS

As he threads his way down the line of wagons. Mormons are stripping their wagons of all but the most essential items. As he passes Mrs. Ledyard, she is surrounded by a welter of discarded household articles. Among them is a dressmaker's dummy at least eight sizes smaller than she is. Mr. Peachtree, obviously in love with the dummy's figure, stares at it wistfully. It is apparent that Mrs. Ledyard has been telling Peachtree of her former beauty.

89

MRS. LEDYARD: *(eyeing the dummy fondly)* ...and I had the smallest waist! Why, my first husband could put his two hands all the way...

Suiting the action to her words, Mrs. Ledyard thoughtlessly starts to girdle her ample waist with both hands. They fail to meet by at least a yard. Mr. Peachtree shakes his head sadly.

At the next wagon, Brother Bolton stands wistfully gazing at an accordion—obviously considering its abandonment. Wiggs pauses.

WIGGS: We'll need music, Brother Bolton...

Bolton smiles his gratitude and Wiggs continues.

At the Jamison wagon, a carefully quilted mirror leans against a wheel while Jamison hauls an infant's cradle across the tailgate. He hesitates, looking at his pregnant wife.

JAMISON: I could make another, Mary.

MRS. JAMISON: *(smiling as she shakes her head)* Doubt you'll have time...

She takes the quilt from the mirror and sets it down tenderly.

MRS. JAMISON: Guess I can do without that mirror, though.

Wiggs pats her shoulder in passing and continues on.

ANOTHER ANGLE—ON JAMISON WAGON

Young Billy Jamison stands wide-eyed as Travis slips the loaded gun into the waistband of his pants, out of sight under his coat. Travis turns and starts hurriedly away at the sound of Sandy's voice calling his name.

SANDY: *(off-screen)* Travis!

FULL SHOT—THE DUGWAY

The Mormons have completed their job. They stand aside, leaning on shovels and picks. A groove has been cut lengthwise across the ledge. As Travis approaches, Jackson faces him.

JACKSON: That the way you wanted it?

Travis nods.

JACKSON: I'll take the first wagon over.

TRAVIS: I was figgerin' on doin' that myself.

WIGGS: *(hurrying up)* I'll lead out...

90

They all turn and give way at the sound of a new, and authoritative voice—the professor's.

HALL: *(off-screen)* Stand aside, gentlemen!

FULL SHOT—PAST TRAVIS AND GROUP TO THE MEDICINE WAGON AS IT APPROACHES

With its horses in single file and Hall on the box, the medicine wagon moves steadily toward the ledge. Denver and Florey, both apprehensive, walk alongside. Wiggs moves out to try and stop it.

WIGGS: Now hold on, Professor!

Florey runs up beside Wiggs—as if sharing his entreaty.

HALL: *(with dignity)* No arguments, please! *(with an air)* This wagon contains nothing of value... its driver included.

FLOREY: *(ready to cry)* Gus!

WIGGS: *(touched—protesting)* But see here, Doc...

HALL: *(impatiently)* Please don't clutter the exit! Lead on, Travis!

Florey runs up beside him.

FLOREY: I'm going with you!

FULL SHOT—LEDGE

Travis takes the lead lines and starts guiding the team out onto the ledge as Florey climbs up beside Hall. The other Mormons move around to help steady the wagon and guide its wheels into the dugway.

MEDIUM CLOSE—WAGON BOX

As Florey settles beside Hall. She is between tears and laughter. The wagon starts to move.

FLOREY: Oh, Gus! You big ham!

HALL: No doubt... *(with professional pride)* But you'll have to admit I read the line well!

She clings to his arm, laughing almost hysterically up at him, but both expressions change to one of fear and tension as the wagon lurches—the first wheel going into the dugway.

ANOTHER ANGLE—CLOSE ON THE DUGWAY
As the first wheel locks into the groove. Mormons are steadying the wagon, holding it. The second wheel drops in.

FULL SHOT—WAGON—MOVING
The wheels in the groove, the wagon is canted perilously on one side—with the far set of wheels turning in empty air, projecting out over the ledge.

MEDIUM CLOSE—WAGON BOX
Florey takes one look over the edge, then closes her eyes and clings fearfully to Hall's arm. Beneath them is empty space. The wagon balances precariously, like a tight-rope walker.

ANGLE ON MORMON GROUP
Their faces tense as they watch the progress of the wagon.

ANGLE FROM WITHIN WAGON
Shooting past Hall and Florey toward Travis as he carefully guides the horses along the ledge, steadying them, calling encouragingly.

ANOTHER ANGLE ON LEDGE CROSSING
Shooting from behind Travis, past the horses, toward the rocking wagon. It sways and seems about to break out of the dugway, but Travis moves the horses faster—pulls them onto the far side—and the wagon swings safely back to four wheels as the Mormons on the far side let out a yell of triumph.

MEDIUM CLOSE—WAGON BOX
Florey and Hall can at first scarcely believe they have made the crossing successfully. She throws her arms around him. He pats her awkwardly. But he is listening to the cheers of the Mormons.

HALL: There, there, Florey...it's all over...
Travis comes up and stands at the edge of the seat.
TRAVIS: *(indicating Mormons with a wave of his hand)* They're giving you quite a hand, Doc.
HALL: Well, they needn't expect an encore!

Travis laughs and starts away, to recross the ledge, but has to step aside as Floyd rides past him, scouting the way ahead. Travis looks after him with concern, but has to return to go about the task of getting the other wagons across.

WIPE TO:

ANGLE ON PERKINS WAGON
As it waits to cross the dugway. Wiggs stands beside Perkins. Prudence sits beside her father.
WIGGS: Still of the same mind about our Gentiles, Adam?
PERKINS: No, Jonathan . . . I was wrong. But the Lord's opened my eyes.
He turns to Prudence.
PERKINS: It's a lesson to us both, daughter.
WIGGS: *(smiling)* Don't read her any lessons, Adam. Her eyes were open all along.
TRAVIS: *(off-screen)* Next wagon!
PERKINS: *(gathering up reins)* That's us . . .
As the Perkins wagon moves out, the grain wagon—driven by Sam Jackson—takes its place. It is the last wagon to go.

ANGLE ON THE CLEGGS—NEAR LEDGE
Shiloh waits with Reese and Jesse as Floyd rides in and dismounts.
FLOYD: *(eagerly)* It's a clear trail from here on down . . . You can see the San Juan River from just ahead.
Shiloh looks at his boys with satisfaction and his lips curl in a wolfish smile.
SHILOH: Then it might as well be now!
He walks away from the ledge toward the grain wagon, with his boys following.

WIDE ANGLE
As the four Cleggs walk toward the waiting grain wagon. All the Mormons are on the far side of the ledge, having safely crossed their wagons. Possibly the Perkins wagon can be seen entering the dugway. Wiggs stands near the grain wagon on which Sam Jackson

93

is sitting. Sandy and Travis are completing the final adjustment of the team's harness.

TRAVIS: *(calling)* All ready, Mister Jackson!

SHILOH: *(countermanding it)* Not yet...

ANOTHER ANGLE—CLOSER ON GRAIN WAGON

Wiggs and the boys turn as the Cleggs purposefully come nearer.

SHILOH: We're sayin' goodbye, Elder... We're partin' company.

Wiggs and the others stare, knowing there is more behind Shiloh's words.

SHILOH: You been real good to us Cleggses... Reese now... he ain't goin' to forget you... None of us apt to... So it's only fittin we give *you* somethin' to remember us by...

He looks at the grain wagon.

SHILOH: *(with a grin for Wiggs—as he indicates the grain wagon)* More val-able than gold itself?... You said so, Elder!... YOU!

He points at Sam Jackson.

SHILOH: Get down off'n there!

JACKSON: Why? What are you going to do?

The sentence is barely out of Jackson's mouth when Shiloh draws and fires. Jackson stares in wonder, his hand going to his chest and coming away with bloody fingers. He starts to stand, to protest, then lurches out of the seat and topples to the ground.

Sandy and Travis cannot move. Jesse's shotgun covers them both at murderous range.

SHILOH: *(his gun covering Wiggs)* You, Elder... git up there...

Wiggs slowly climbs up.

SHILOH: *(vindictively)* And to save you askin' why, I'll tell you... You're goin' to have the privilege of takin' the grain over yourself...

Wiggs gingerly picks up the reins, and looks ahead.

REVERSE ANGLE—FROM WIGGS'S POINT OF VIEW

Over the backs of the horses toward the narrow ledge. Shiloh stands near the wagon seat, on the opposite side from Travis.

SHILOH: Only it's going to be at a dead run!... and the wheels ain't goin' to be set in that groove!

CLOSE ON WIGGS
Wiggs's lips tighten as he hears his death sentence—and worse, the destruction of the grain and the failure of his mission.

MEDIUM CLOSE—SHILOH AND FLOYD
SHILOH: *(gesturing off)* Jesse—Floyd—stand back! Give the elder some room...
He turns and hands his quirt to Reese.
SHILOH: Reese, I'll let you whip up them horses...
As Reese takes the quirt and steps forward with a hellish grin...
TRAVIS: *(quietly)* Drop it, Reese!

REVERSE ANGLE
Favoring Travis as he stands in front of the lead horse. He has thrown back his coat, revealing the pistol shoved into the waistband of his trousers.
TRAVIS: *(still quietly)* You heard me!

WIDER ANGLE
Floyd is the first of the Cleggs to recover and go into action. Stepping in front of Jesse to face Travis, his hands flash to his guns, but Travis beats him to the draw and fires twice. Floyd drops. Jesse raises his shotgun only to be tackled by Sandy who flings himself upon him and the two men stagger back to the side of the mountain, locked in a struggle for the shotgun.

Shiloh fires at Travis, who flings himself full on the ground, but snaps a shot at Reese—who was trying to draw a bead on him with his rifle.

Shiloh takes cover behind one of the wagon wheels on the side opposite Travis, but unable to get a shot at him through the legs of the horses. He turns his attention to Jesse and Sandy, still struggling for the shotgun.

Jesse, with his superior weight and strength, is giving Sandy a beating. Sandy's back is to Shiloh. Jesse has the shotgun crosswise across his neck—thrusting it up and back, in spite of Sandy's efforts to hang on.

Jesse brings up his knee into Sandy's groin and then with an upward jerk of the shotgun, sends him sprawling on the ground...just as Shiloh fires at what had been the clear target of Sandy's back. Jesse gets the shot in the stomach and, with a bewildered expression, pitches forward on his face.

Shiloh stands and gapes and almost numbly takes a few steps forward, staring at the last of his boys. Sandy sprawls on the ground, twisted with pain, exhausted and unable to reach the shotgun on the ground near him.

Travis comes from behind the horses, covering Shiloh with his pistol.

TRAVIS: Drop your gun, Mister Clegg!

CLOSER SHOT

Shiloh seems not to hear him, so lost is he in the tragedy that has befallen the Cleggs.

SHILOH: *(sobbing)* My boys... You killed my boys... Good boys they was...

TRAVIS: I'm askin' you to drop your gun!

SHILOH: *(whiningly)* Sure... I'm whipped... I know when I'm whipped...

He starts to turn, his hands slowly coming up as if in a gesture of surrender. He presents the picture of a defeated, harmless old man. But as he completes his turn, his gun hand leaps up—but not quick enough. Travis fires twice—the first shot failing to stop Shiloh as he tries to fire back. The second does it. Shiloh falls—hands digging into the dust.

Travis slowly turns and looks up at Wiggs.

ANOTHER ANGLE

Revealing Wiggs, still perched on the wagon box. He is looking at the dead men, at Sandy slowly and groggily getting to his feet, at Travis with the gun at his side.

WIGGS: *(in hushed tones)* And I thought you never drew on a man...?

TRAVIS: *(quietly)* That's right, sir... Only on snakes!

REVERSE ANGLE
As Travis turns and starts away, followed by Sandy, the Mormons come running across the ledge. Prudence and Denver are among the first, each with fear and anxiety in her eyes.
Prudence doesn't hesitate when she sees Sandy, but runs to him. Denver slows when she sees Travis; and, with a shyness new and strange to her, cannot take another step. She must wait for him to come to her.

CLOSER ANGLE—TRAVIS AND DENVER
As Travis joins her. He holds out his hand for one of hers.
TRAVIS: I needed that extra bullet!

DISSOLVE

DAY—THE ARCHES
It is either the same day or the next, and the Mormons stand grouped under vaulting, cathedral-like arches of stone. Five rock cairns mark the graves of the four Cleggs and of Sam Jackson. Wiggs stands bareheaded before them, his face raised in prayer or sermon.
WIGGS: He was a good man—Brother Jackson was—maybe a mite quick to anger, but that's a manly failing... And now, as to these Cleggs...
He pauses, sorting his words.
WIGGS: I can't give 'em much of a recommend and that's the truth, Lord... But it's not for us to judge them. This I will say: Sometimes we need the evil to bring out the good... For a man never knows his strength until it's put to the test... Amen.
As he turns from the cairns, the Mormons raise their voices in that stout hymn, "All Is Well." But after the first few bars, Wiggs turns to Travis.
WIGGS: *(calling)* Lead out, BROTHER Travis.
And the Mormons, still singing, make for their wagons as Travis rides through an arch, pauses, and makes a sweeping forward gesture with his arm... And as the first of the wagons clatters through the arch behind him:

WIDE SWEEPING PANORAMA OF A BEAUTIFUL GREEN VALLEY

(It is to be hoped that the cinematographer may find a valley with a winding brook, lush grass, the very picture of a pastoral Eden and a worthy goal for this Mormon migration.)

From behind the camera, in this scene, roll the Mormon wagons— men, women, and children walking beside their teams—still singing "All Is Well."

ANOTHER ANGLE

On Travis walking arm-in-arm with Denver—leading his horse. Behind him, trying his best to step into the long-legged Texan's bootprints, proudly walks Billy Jamison. Teddy, the dog, cuts excited capers through the tall grass.

ANOTHER ANGLE—THE GRAIN WAGON

Mrs. Ledyard drives, while Elder Wiggs leads the team. He comes to a stop at a point commanding a view of his valley and as the grain wagon continues past he looks happily from the bulging sacks to the fields below, seeing in his mind's eye the four-square Mormon blocks, the lines of Mormon poplars, the communal fields, and the sturdy houses that will be built.

He is so lost in his reverie that he does not at first heed the appearance of the professor and Florey, who come up beside him. Florey smiles—guessing at the elder's thoughts.

FLOREY: *(lightly)* What are you doing, Elder—laying out the streets and the town hall?

Wiggs starts at her voice, then smiles.

WIGGS: Yep, and the schoolhouse, too!...

He is struck by a sudden thought.

WIGGS: Doc, why don't you and Miss Florey stay with us? You've *earned* a place in this valley!... Why, you could farm a piece o' land, or teach school, or... *(with utter sincerity)* You'd be most welcome.

Florey looks at Hall with swift hope that possibly now, at long last, she may realize her dream of a home. Hall is deeply touched, but realizes the life is not for him.

HALL: No, Elder... it's kind of you to want us, but we'd only be in the way.

He takes Florey's hand, now speaking theatrically.

HALL: Besides, Miss Phyffe and I have decided to return to the Theatah! A month hence we open in Santa Fe. "The Three Musketeers"... I, of course, shall play young d'Artagnan...

Wiggs knows how disappointed Florey is and looks at her with understanding. Impulsively she kisses him on the cheek. Her eyes are suspiciously bright.

FLOREY: But there is one thing you can do for us!

She looks meaningfully at the professor.

HALL: *(a little sheepish)* Ah, yes... *(he clears his throat)* Miss Phyffe and I feel that we have been... ah... engaged long enough.

FLOREY: *(nodding)* Twelve years.

HALL: I've never believed in long engagements, so I think the time has come...

WIGGS: *(explosively)* Well, I'll be go to...!

HALL: *(shocked)* Why, Elder!

The singing of "All Is Well" swells as we—

FADE OUT.

THE END